Paleo Instant Pot Cookbook

Easy and Delicious Paleo Recipes for Your Instant Pot

Lindsey Page

Table of Contents

Introduction

The Instant Pot will revolutionize your cooking experience forever. It is a programmable electric pressure cooker that can be used as a slow cooker, rice cooker and steamer. It is also designed to make yogurt, sauté and brown vegetables and meats, and keep meals warm. Using an Instant Pot, you can prepare delicious meals in less than 15 minutes. There's no need to spend hours in the kitchen, standing over multiple pots and pans.

The Paleo diet is inspired by the diet of our ancestors during the caveman era. Supported by medical and scientific research, the diet is all about eating healthy foods and staying away from processed foods and artificial sweeteners. It takes you back to the days of our primitive ancestors who did not have to worry about diseases such as obesity and diabetes. That's because they ate whatever they found; foods that were naturally abundant.

If you follow the Paleo diet, learning to prepare Paleo recipes is an important step towards achieving your goals. In this book, you will find 91 easy and delicious Paleo Instant Pot recipes for breakfast, soups and stews, poultry, meats, seafood, vegetables and dessert.

CHAPTER ONE
Breakfast

Breakfast Casserole

Yield: 3 servings
Preparation Time: 15 minutes
Cooking Time: 25 minutes
Total Time: 40 minutes
Ingredients:
2 teaspoons coconut oil
2 breakfast sausages, discard casing
1 medium onion, chopped
1 large clove garlic, minced
1 cup cauliflower, riced
4 button mushrooms, sliced
1 medium bell pepper, deseeded and diced
6 eggs, beaten
½ cup coconut milk
Salt and pepper to taste
1 green onion, thinly sliced

Directions:
1. Spread the cauliflower over the bottom of a heatproof dish.
2. Set your Instant Pot to SAUTÉ. Heat the coconut oil.
3. Add sausages, garlic, and onions. Break the sausages with a wooden spoon, and sauté until they are brown.
4. Press CANCEL. Transfer the mixture to the heatproof dish.
5. Place a layer of mushrooms followed by bell pepper.
6. In a bowl, whisk together the eggs, coconut milk, salt and pepper. Pour over the sausages. Cover the dish with foil.

7. Pour 1½ cups water into the bottom of the Instant Pot. Add a steamer rack and place the dish on the rack.

8. Close the lid, press MANUAL, and cook at high pressure for 20 minutes.

7. When the cooking is complete, do a natural pressure release for 10 minutes. Quick release the remaining pressure.

Nutritional Information (Per Serving)
Calories: 349
Fat: 26.7 g
Sat Fat: 15.4 g
Carbohydrates: 12.6 g
Fiber: 3.4 g
Sugar: 6.9 g
Protein: 17.9 g

Breakfast Pie

Yield: 8 servings
Preparation Time: 15 minutes
Cooking Time: 10 minutes
Total Time: 25 minutes
Ingredients:
12 eggs, whisked
1½ pounds breakfast pork sausages, broken
2 sweet potatoes, shredded
1 ½ tablespoons garlic powder
1 large green bell pepper, chopped
2 onions, chopped
1 cup yellow squash, chopped
3 teaspoons dried basil
Salt and pepper to taste
Coconut oil to grease, melted

Directions:

1. Grease a heatproof dish with coconut oil.

2. Add all the ingredients into the dish and stir. Cover the dish with foil.

3. Pour 1½ cups water into the Instant Pot. Place a trivet in the pot. Place the dish on the trivet.

4. Close the lid, press MANUAL, and cook at high pressure for 20 minutes.

5. When the cooking is complete, do a natural pressure release.

6. Slice and serve warm.

Nutritional Information (Per Serving)
Calories: 416
Fat: 24.1 g
Sat Fat: 8.1 g
Carbohydrates: 27.5 g
Fiber: 4.2 g
Sugar: 3.4 g
Protein: 23.9 g

Eggs with Salsa

Yield: 2 servings
Preparation Time: 15 minutes
Cooking Time: 20 minutes
Total Time: 35 minutes
Ingredients:
¾ cup tomato salsa
2 eggs
Salt and pepper to taste
1 tablespoon fresh cilantro, chopped

Directions:
1. Lightly grease 2 ramekins.
2. Divide the salsa between the ramekins.
3. Crack 1 egg in each ramekin over salsa. Sprinkle with salt and pepper.
4. Cover the ramekins with foil.
5. At the bottom of the Instant pot, arrange a steamer trivet and pour 1½ cups of water. Place the ramekins on top of the trivet.
6. Close the lid, select MANUAL, and cook at low pressure for 20 minutes.
7. When the cooking is complete, do a quick pressure release.
8. Serve warm with the garnishing of cilantro.

Nutritional Information (Per Serving)
Calories: 111
Fat: 4.4 g
Sat Fat: 7.8 g
Carbohydrates: 9.4 g
Fiber: 0 g
Sugar: 3.3 g
Protein: 5.6 g
Sodium: 600 mg

Salmon & Egg Cups

Yield: 4 servings
Preparation Time: 15 minutes
Cooking Time: 4 minutes
Total Time: 19 minutes
Ingredients:
1½ cups cooked salmon, chopped
2 tablespoons fresh parsley, minced
4 eggs
2 tablespoons coconut cream
Salt and pepper to taste

Directions:
1. Lightly grease 4 ramekins. Keep aside.
2. In a bowl, mix together salmon and parsley.
3. Divide the salmon mixture in each prepared ramekin evenly.
4. Carefully, crack 1 egg in each ramekin over salmon mixture.
5. Top the eggs with coconut cream evenly and sprinkle with salt and pepper. (For a hard yolk keep the ramekins uncovered but for soft egg yolk, cover tightly with a foil paper).
6. At the bottom of the Instant Pot, arrange a steamer trivet and pour 1 cup of water.
7. Place the ramekins on top of the trivet.
8. Close the lid, select MANUAL, and cook at low pressure for 4 minutes.
9. When the cooking is complete, do a quick pressure release.
10. Serve warm.

Nutritional Information (Per Serving)
Calories: 193
Fat: 11.4 g

Sat Fat: 3.7 g
Carbohydrates: 0.9 g
Fiber: 0.2 g
Sugar: 0.6 g
Protein: 22.3 g
Sodium: 140 mg

Scallion Omelet Cups

Yield: 2 servings
Preparation Time: 15 minutes
Cooking Time: 5 minutes
Total Time: 20 minutes
Ingredients:
3 eggs
¾ cup water
⅛ teaspoon garlic powder
⅛ teaspoon red pepper flakes, crushed
Salt and pepper to taste
2 scallions, chopped
Pinch of sesame seeds

Directions:
1. At the bottom of the Instant Pot, arrange a steamer trivet and pour 1 cup of water.

2. In a bowl, add eggs, water, garlic powder, red pepper flakes, salt and pepper and beat until well combined.

3. Stir in scallion and sesame seeds.

4. Transfer egg mixture into 2 heatproof bowls. Place the bowls on top of the trivet.

5. Close the lid, select MANUAL, and cook at high pressure for 5 minutes.

6. When the cooking is complete, do a natural pressure release for 10 minutes. Quick release the remaining pressure.

7. Serve immediately.

Nutritional Information (Per Serving)
Calories: 101
Fat: 6.7 g
Sat Fat: 2.1 g
Carbohydrates: 1.9 g
Fiber: 0.5 g
Sugar: 0.9 g
Protein: 8.7 g
Sodium: 175 mg

Zucchini and Sweet Potato Frittata

Yield: 6 servings
Preparation Time: 15 minutes
Cooking Time: 12 minutes
Total Time: 27 minutes
Ingredients:
1½ tablespoons coconut oil, melted
2 medium sweet potatoes, peeled and chopped into slices
3 zucchinis, sliced
2 medium red bell peppers, sliced
3 tablespoons fresh parsley, chopped
12 eggs, whisked
Salt and pepper to taste

Directions:
1. Grease the inside of a heatproof dish with coconut oil.
2. Place the sweet potatoes in the dish.
3. Place a layer of zucchini followed by bell pepper.
4. Add salt and pepper to the whisked eggs and pour over the vegetables.
5. Pour 1½ cups water in the Instant Pot. Place a steamer rack in it and place the dish over the rack.
6. Close the lid and select STEAM. Cook for 12 minutes.
7. Preheat the oven broiler.
8. When the cooking is complete, do a quick pressure release.
9. Broil in the oven for a few minutes.
10. Garnish with parsley. Cut into 6 equal wedges and serve.

Nutritional Information (Per Serving)
Calories: 306
Fat: 21.5 g
Sat Fat: 13.6 g
Carbohydrates: 18.1 g
Fiber: 3 g

Sugar: 6.7 g
Protein: 13.4 g

Chicken & Sweet Potato Casserole

Yield: 4 servings
Preparation Time: 15 minutes
Cooking Time: 13 minutes
Total Time: 28 minutes
Ingredients:
4 eggs
1 tablespoon water
¾ teaspoon taco seasoning
¼ teaspoon red chili powder
Salt to taste
6 ounces cooked chicken, cubed
2 pounds sweet potatoes, peeled and cubed
¼ cup onion, chopped
1 jalapeño pepper, chopped

Directions:
1. At the bottom of Instant Pot, arrange a steamer trivet and pour 1 cup of water.

2. In a heatproof bowl, add eggs, water, taco seasonings, chili powder and salt and beat until well combined.

3. Add chicken, sweet potatoes, onion and jalapeño pepper and stir to combine.

4. With a piece of foil, cover the bowl and place on top of the trivet.

5. Close the lid, select MANUAL, and cook at high pressure for 13 minutes.

6. When the cooking is complete, use a natural pressure release.

7. Serve warm.

Nutritional Information (Per Serving)
Calories: 402
Fat: 6.1 g
Sat Fat: 1.8 g
Carbohydrates: 65 g
Fiber: 9.6 g
Sugar: 2 g
Protein: 21.5 g
Sodium: 202 mg

Butternut Squash 'N' Oatmeal

Yield: 6 servings
Preparation Time: 15 minutes
Cooking Time: 15 minutes
Total Time: 30 minutes
Ingredients:
1 cup walnuts + extra for topping
1 cup almonds + extra for topping
2 medium butternut squashes, peeled, deseeded and cubed
2 teaspoons cinnamon powder
2 cups coconut milk + extra for topping
A handful currants, to top
4 apples, cored, peeled and chopped into pieces
2 tablespoons coconut sugar or to taste (optional)
2 tablespoons desiccated coconut
½ teaspoon nutmeg powder
Maple syrup for topping (optional)
A large pinch salt

Directions:
1. Soak the almonds and walnuts in a bowl of water. Add salt and soak for about 10 – 12 hours.

2. Drain and blend in a blender until smooth.

3. Add the blended nuts and rest of the ingredients (except the toppings) into the Instant Pot. Mix well.

4. Cover and select PORRIDGE option for 15 minutes. Let the pressure release naturally.

5. Open the lid, and mash the ingredients with a potato masher.

6. Top with coconut milk, nuts, currants, desiccated coconut and maple syrup if desired and serve.

Nutritional Information (Per Serving)

Calories: 458
Fat: 39.8 g
Sat Fat: 18.6 g
Carbohydrates: 22.9 g
Fiber: 7.5 g
Sugar: 10.6 g
Protein: 10.8 g
Sodium: 222 mg

Sweet Potato Bread

Yield: 8 servings
Preparation Time: 15 minutes
Cooking Time: 20 minutes
Total Time: 35 minutes
Ingredients:
1¼ cups blanched almond flour
½ cup tapioca flour
¼ cup coconut flour
¼ cup coconut sugar
1 teaspoon baking soda
2 teaspoons ground cinnamon
1 teaspoon pumpkin pie spice
½ teaspoon salt
3 organic eggs
½ cup unsweetened almond milk
½ cup homemade sweet potato puree
2 tablespoons coconut oil
1 teaspoon apple cider vinegar
⅓ cup walnuts, chopped

Directions:
1. Line a 3½x7 ½-inch loaf pan with parchment paper. Keep aside.

2. In a large bowl, mix together flours, coconut sugar, baking soda, spices and salt.

3. Add eggs, almond milk, sweet potato puree, coconut oil and vinegar and beat until smooth.

4. Gently, fold in walnuts.

5. Place the mixture into prepared loaf pan evenly. With a piece of foil, cover the loaf pan.

6. At the bottom of Instant Pot, arrange a steamer trivet and pour 2 cups of water.

7. Place the bread pan on top of the trivet.

8. Close the lid, select MANUAL, and cook at high pressure for 30 minutes.

9. When the cooking is complete, use a natural pressure release.

10. Remove the lid and transfer the bread pan onto a wire rack to cool completely before slicing.

11. Cut into desired sized slices and serve.

Nutritional Information (Per Serving)
Calories: 407
Fat: 26.7 g
Sat Fat: 5.1 g
Carbohydrates: 31.5 g
Fiber: 5.5 g
Sugar: 7 g
Protein: 12 g
Sodium: 360 mg

Veggie Hash

Yield: 3 servings
Preparation Time: 15 minutes
Cooking Time: 8 minutes
Total Time: 23 minutes
Ingredients:
2 cups sweet potato, peeled and chopped
1 cup bell pepper, seeded and chopped
1 medium onion, chopped
1 garlic clove, minced
1 tablespoon olive oil
Salt and pepper to taste
1 teaspoon ground cumin
1 teaspoon paprika
Pinch of cayenne
½ cup water

Directions:
1. In the pot of Instant Pot, mix together all ingredients.
2. Close the lid, select MANUAL, and cook at high pressure for 1 minutes.
3. When the cooking is complete, press CANCEL and do a natural pressure release.
4. Remove the lid and select SAUTÉ.
5. Cook for 6–8 minutes, stirring occasionally.
6. Press CANCEL and serve hot.

Nutritional Information (Per Serving)
Calories: 194
Fat: 5.7 g
Sat Fat: 0.7 g
Carbohydrates: 35.1 g
Fiber: 6.1 g
Sugar: 12 g

Protein: 3.8 g
Sodium: 104 mg

Maple Apple

Yield: 6 servings
Preparation Time: 15 minutes
Cooking Time: 15 minutes
Total Time: 30 minutes
Ingredients:
1½ pounds apples, cored and chopped
½ tablespoon ground cinnamon
⅛ teaspoon ground nutmeg
A pinch sea salt
Juice of ½ lemon
½ teaspoon ground allspice
½ teaspoon ginger powder
½ teaspoon ground cloves
¼ cup maple syrup
¾ cup water

Directions:
1. Add all the ingredients into the Instant Pot.
2. Cover and select MANUAL. Cook at high pressure for 5 minutes. Let the pressure release naturally.
3. Select SAUTÉ, and simmer until the apples are reduced to half in volume. The color of the mixture will be brown.
4. Cool for a while and blend with an immersion blender until smooth.
5. Pour into glass jars. Fasten the lid and refrigerate until use. It can last for 2 weeks.

Nutritional Information (Per Serving)

Calories: 148
Fat: 0.7 g
Sat Fat: 0.1 g
Carbohydrates: 38.8 g
Fiber: 5.5 g
Sugar: 30.2 g
Protein: 0.7 g
Sodium: 43 mg

Sweet Potato Hash

Yield: 4 servings
Preparation Time: 15 minutes
Cooking Time: 10 minutes
Total Time: 25 minutes
Ingredients:
2 medium yellow bell peppers, chopped
2 medium orange bell peppers, chopped
4 cups sweet potatoes, cubed
½ pound butternut squash, peeled and cubed
4 tomatoes, thinly sliced
2 teaspoons garlic, minced
2 teaspoons mustard powder
4 tablespoons coconut oil
2 teaspoons thyme
½ cup water
Salt and pepper to taste

Directions:
1. Add all the ingredients into the Instant Pot and stir.
2. Close the lid, select MANUAL, and cook at high pressure for 10 minutes.
3. When the cooking is complete, use a natural pressure release.

Nutritional Information (Per Serving)
Calories: 377
Fat: 14.9 g
Sat Fat: 12 g
Carbohydrates: 60.1 g
Fiber: 11.2 g
Sugar: 8.2 g
Protein: 5.5 g

Breakfast Meatloaf

Yield: 8 servings
Preparation Time: 10 minutes
Cooking Time: 40 minutes
Total Time: 50 minutes
Ingredients:
1½ tablespoons coconut oil
3 pounds ground pork
5 cloves garlic, minced
1½ teaspoons crushed red pepper flakes
⅓ cup almond flour
1 large onion, minced
2 teaspoons sea salt
A handful fresh sage, minced
1½ teaspoons marjoram
3 eggs
1½ teaspoons dried oregano
1½ tablespoons smoked paprika

Directions:
1. Place a skillet over medium high heat. Add oil. When the oil is melted, add onion and sauté until translucent.

2. Add the garlic and sauté until fragrant. Turn off the heat.

3. Transfer into a large bowl. Add rest of the ingredients into the bowl and mix well using your hands. Do not mix for long, as the meat tends to get tough.

4. Grease a loaf pan that fits inside your Instant Pot. Transfer the meat mixture to the loaf pan and press firmly.

5. Pour 1½ cups water into your Instant Pot and lower a trivet.

6. Place the loaf pan on the trivet and close the lid.

7. Set the Instant Pot to MANUAL and cook at high pressure for 30 minutes.

8. Let the pressure release naturally for 10 minutes. Quick release the remaining pressure.

9. Slowly remove the meat. Serve hot.

10. Leftovers can be stored in an airtight container.

11. To reheat, heat on a skillet with a little oil.

Nutritional Information (Per Serving)
Calories: 387
Fat: 18.5 g
Sat Fat: 10.9 g
Carbohydrates: 7.2 g
Fiber: 3.4 g
Sugar: 1.6 g
Protein: 48.2 g
Sodium: 592 mg

Kale Casserole

Yield: 4 servings
Preparation Time: 10 minutes
Cooking Time: 20 minutes
Total Time: 30 minutes
Ingredients:
½ pounds bacon, cooked and chopped
2½ cups fresh kale, trimmed and chopped
1 small yellow onion, chopped
6 eggs
Salt and pepper to taste

Directions:
1. In a large bowl, add eggs, salt, and pepper and beat until well combined.
2. Add remaining ingredients and mix well.
3. Place the mixture into a baking dish.
4. At the bottom of Instant Pot, arrange a steamer trivet and add 1 cup of water.
5. Place the baking dish on top of the trivet and close the lid.
6. Set the Instant Pot to MANUAL and cook at high pressure for 20 minutes.
7. Release the pressure naturally.
8. Serve warm.

Nutritional Information (Per Serving)
Calories: 429
Fat: 30.3 g
Sat Fat: 9.8 g
Carbohydrates: 7.3 g
Fiber: 1 g
Sugar: 1.3 g
Protein: 30.7 g

Zucchini Banana Bread

Yield: 8 servings
Preparation Time: 10 minutes
Cooking Time: 40 minutes
Total Time: 50 minutes
Ingredients:
1 cup coconut flour
4 teaspoons vanilla extract
2 teaspoons orange zest
3 teaspoons baking soda
1 teaspoon sea salt
2 tablespoons ground cinnamon
2 cups zucchini, finely grated
3 cups mashed bananas
½ cup coconut oil, softened (do not melt)
1 cup walnuts, chopped (optional)

Directions:
1. Add oil, zest, vanilla, cinnamon and banana to a bowl and beat with a beater until smooth and creamy.

2. Add coconut flour, baking soda and salt. Whisk until well combined. Add zucchini and walnuts if using and stir.

3. Pour the batter into a greased bread pan (fill it 2/3 full). Cook in batches if necessary. Cover the pan with foil.

4. Pour 2 cups water into the Instant Pot. Place a steamer rack in it. Place the pan on the rack.

5. Close the lid, select MANUAL, and cook at high pressure for 40 minutes.

6. Let the pressure release naturally.

7. Run a knife along the sides of the bread to loosen the edges. Invert onto a plate.

8. Let it cool completely. Slice and serve.

Nutritional Information (Per Serving)
Calories: 399
Fat: 26.1 g
Sat Fat: 14.4 g
Carbohydrates: 37.1 g
Fiber: 15.8 g
Sugar: 7.9 g
Protein: 8.8 g
Sodium: 711 mg

CHAPTER TWO

Soups, Chilis and Stews

Chicken & Kale Soup

Yield: 4 servings
Preparation Time: 15 minutes
Cooking Time: 12 minutes
Total Time: 27 minutes
Ingredients:
2 tablespoons olive oil
3 celery stalks, chopped
3 large carrots, peeled and chopped
1 small yellow onion, chopped
¼ teaspoon dried oregano, crushed
¼ teaspoon dried thyme, crushed
Salt and pepper to taste
4 cups homemade chicken broth
1 cup water
1 pound cooked chicken, shredded
2 cups fresh kale, trimmed and chopped

Directions:
1. Place the oil in the Instant Pot and select SAUTÉ. Add the celery, carrot and onion and cook for about 5 minutes.
2. Add herbs and pepper and cook for about 1 minute.
3. Press CANCEL and stir in the broth and water.
4. Close the lid, select MANUAL, and cook at high pressure for 4 minutes.
5. When the cooking is complete, do a quick pressure release.
6. Remove the lid and stir in the chicken and kale.

7. Select SAUTÉ and cook for 1–2 minutes more.

8. Serve immediately.

Nutritional Information (Per Serving)
Calories: 318
Fat: 11.9 g
Sat Fat: 2.4 g
Carbohydrates: 11.8 g
Fiber: 2.5 g
Sugar: 4.3 g
Protein: 39.5 g
Sodium: 900 mg

Mexican Chicken Soup

Yield: 3 servings
Preparation Time: 15 minutes
Cooking Time: 30 minutes
Total Time: 45 minutes
Ingredients:
½ pound chicken breast, skinless and boneless
1 can (14.5 ounces) diced tomatoes
2 cups chicken broth
¾ cup celery, chopped
1 medium carrot, peeled and sliced
1 medium onion, chopped
½ cup red bell pepper, chopped
2 large cloves garlic, thinly sliced
1 cup water
2 tablespoons tomato paste
¼ teaspoon chili powder
½ teaspoon cumin
½ teaspoon sea salt
Juice of ½ lemon

¼ cup cilantro, chopped

Directions:

1. Add all the ingredients except lime juice and cilantro into the Instant Pot.

2. Stir, cover and select SOUP option and set the cooking time for 15 minutes at high pressure.

3. When the cooking is complete, let the pressure release naturally.

4. Remove the chicken pieces from the pot. When cool enough to handle, shred the chicken with two forks.

5. Add the shredded chicken back into the pot. Add lime juice and cilantro.

6. Select SAUTÉ and simmer for 10–15 minutes.

7. Serve hot.

Nutritional Information (Per Serving)
Calories: 173
Fat: 3.3 g
Sat Fat: 0.3 g
Carbohydrates: 14.5 g
Fiber: 3.6 g
Sugar: 7.5 g
Protein: 21.6 g
Sodium: 681 mg

Beef & Veggie Soup

Yield: 4 servings
Preparation Time: 15 minutes
Cooking Time: 30 minutes
Total Time: 45 minutes
Ingredients:
1 teaspoon olive oil
1 pound flank steak, trimmed and cubed
3 medium carrots, peeled and chopped
1 large bell pepper, seeded and chopped
1 large celery stalk, chopped
1 onion, chopped
8 ounces fresh mushrooms, sliced
2 cups water
2 cups homemade chicken broth
1 cup tomatoes, crushed
1½ tablespoons fresh oregano, chopped
½ tablespoon dried thyme
1 bay leaf
2 teaspoons garlic powder
Salt to taste

Directions:
1. Place the oil in the Instant Pot and select SAUTÉ. Then add the steak and cook for 6–7 minutes.

2. Add the carrots, bell pepper, celery and onion and cook for 2–3 minutes.

3. Add the mushrooms and cook for 4–5 minutes.

4. Press CANCEL and stir in the remaining ingredients.

5. Close the lid, select SOUP and the default setting.

6. When the cooking is complete, do a quick pressure release.

7. Serve hot.

Pork Soup

Yield: 6 servings
Preparation Time: 15 minutes
Cooking Time: 23 minutes
Total Time: 38 minutes
Ingredients:
2 tablespoons olive oil
½ onion, sliced
6 garlic cloves, minced
1 teaspoon fresh ginger, minced
1 pound pork shoulder, cut into chunks
2 tablespoons apple cider vinegar
2 tablespoons coconut aminos
Salt and pepper to taste
3 cups water
4 cups bok choy, chopped
¼ cup fresh cilantro, chopped

Directions:

1. Place the oil in the Instant Pot and select SAUTÉ. Add the onion, garlic and ginger and cook for 2–3 minutes.

2. Press CANCEL and stir in the remaining ingredients except bok choy and cilantro.

3. Close the lid, select MANUAL, and cook at high pressure for 20 minutes.

4. When the cooking is complete, do a natural pressure release for 10 minutes. Quick release the remaining pressure.

5. Open the lid and stir in the bok choy.

6. Immediately, close the lid and place the pressure valve to SEAL position for about 10 minutes.

7. Remove the lid and serve immediately with the garnishing of cilantro.

Nutritional Information (Per Serving)
Calories: 282
Fat: 21 g
Sat Fat: 6.6 g
Carbohydrates: 4.2 g
Fiber: 0.8 g
Sugar: 1 g
Protein: 18.6 g
Sodium: 120 mg

Squash & Apple Soup

Yield: 4 servings
Preparation Time: 20 minutes
Cooking Time: 18 minutes
Total Time: 38 minutes
Ingredients:

2 teaspoons olive oil

1 small onion, chopped

3 cups butternut squash, peeled and cubed

1 teaspoon fresh ginger, grated finely

1 medium apple, peeled, cored and cubed

2–3 teaspoons curry powder

1 teaspoon cayenne pepper

¼ teaspoon ground turmeric

4 cups homemade vegetable broth

Salt and pepper to taste

1 tablespoon fresh lemon juice

2 tablespoons fresh cilantro, chopped

Directions:

1. Place the oil in the Instant Pot and select SAUTÉ. Add the onion and cook for about 3 minutes.

2. Add the squash and cook for 4–5 minutes.

3. Add the ginger, apple and spices and cook for 1–2 minutes.

4. Press CANCEL and stir in the broth.

5. Close the lid, select MANUAL, and cook at high pressure for 5 minutes.

6. When the cooking is complete, use a natural pressure release.

7. Open the lid and let the soup cool slightly.

8. Using a hand blender, blend the soup until smooth.

9. Stir in salt, pepper and lemon juice.

10. Serve hot with the garnishing of cilantro.

Cozy Rainbow Vegetable Soup

Yield: 4 servings
Preparation Time: 15 minutes
Cooking Time: 5 minutes
Total Time: 20 minutes
Ingredients:
1 cup butternut squash, peeled and diced
½ cup green squash, diced
1 cup red bell pepper, diced
1 medium carrot, diced
2 green onions, chopped + extra to garnish
1 medium onion, chopped
½ cup celery leaves, chopped
1 cup celery stalks, chopped
2 large cloves garlic, sliced
1 tablespoon lemon juice
2 cups water
Salt to taste

Directions:
1. Add all the ingredients except salt and lemon juice into the Instant Pot.

2. Close the lid, select MANUAL, and cook at high pressure for 5 minutes.

3. Let the pressure release naturally.

4. Stir in lemon juice and salt.

5. Ladle into soup bowls. Garnish with green onions and serve.

Nutritional Information (Per Serving)
Calories: 55
Fat: 0.3 g
Sat Fat: 0.1 g
Carbohydrates: 12.8 g
Fiber: 2.9 g
Sugar: 5.1 g
Protein: 1.7 g

Minestrone Soup

Yield: 6 servings
Preparation Time: 15 minutes
Cooking Time: 15 minutes
Total Time: 30 minutes
Ingredients:
1 tablespoon olive oil
1 medium carrot, peeled and diced
1 medium onion, diced
2 cloves garlic, minced
1 zucchini, diced
1 cup fresh spinach, chopped
1 medium sweet potato, peeled and cubed
1 stalk celery, chopped
¾ pound ground pork, crumbled
1 can (14.5 ounces) diced tomatoes
2 cups low sodium vegetable broth
1 cup water
1 bay leaf
½ teaspoon dried basil
½ teaspoon dried parsley
1 teaspoon dried oregano
Sea salt to taste
¼ teaspoon cayenne pepper to taste

Directions:
1. Select SAUTÉ and add the oil. When the oil is heated, add the garlic and onion and stir-fry until onion gets translucent.

2. Add rest of the ingredients except spinach into the Instant Pot. Mix well.

3. Close the lid, select MANUAL, and cook at high pressure for 6 minutes.

4. When the cooking is complete, use a natural pressure release.

5. Add spinach. Mix well. Cover and let it sit for a few minutes until spinach wilts. Discard the bay leaves.

6. Ladle into soup bowls and serve.

Nutritional Information (Per Serving)
Calories: 150
Fat: 4.6 g
Sat Fat: 1 g
Carbohydrates: 11.1 g
Fiber: 2.3 g
Sugar: 4.3 g
Protein: 16.4 g

Vegetable Beef Soup

Yield: 4 servings
Preparation Time: 15 minutes
Cooking Time: 35 minutes
Total Time: 50 minutes
Ingredients:
2 cups beef broth
1 pound chuck roast, cut into 1 inch cubes
2 cups water
2 sweet potatoes, peeled and cubed
8 ounces canned, fire roasted diced tomatoes
½ pound carrots, peeled and sliced
2 stalks celery, sliced thin
1 cup green beans, trimmed
Salt and pepper to taste
1 medium onion, chopped
Meat magic seasoning or any other seasoning of your choice

Directions:
1. Add all the ingredients into the Instant Pot.
2. Stir, cover and select MEAT/STEW. Cook at high pressure for 35 minutes.
3. When the cooking is complete, use a natural pressure release.
4. Ladle the soup into bowls and serve.

Nutritional Information (Per Serving)
Calories: 441
Fat: 10.4 g
Sat Fat: 3.7 g
Carbohydrates: 38.2 g
Fiber: 6.1 g
Sugar: 11.6 g
Protein: 46.6 g

Chicken Chili

Yield: 8 servings
Preparation Time: 15 minutes
Cooking Time: 20 minutes
Total Time: 35 minutes
Ingredients:
4 (6-ounce) grass-fed chicken breasts
4 carrots, peeled and chopped
4 celery stalks, chopped
1 medium yellow onion, chopped
3 garlic cloves, chopped
1 (4-ounce) can diced hatch chilis
1 teaspoon dried oregano
1 teaspoon ground cumin
Salt and pepper to taste
1 cup unsweetened coconut milk
2 cups homemade chicken broth
2 avocados, peeled, pitted and chopped

Directions:
1. In the Instant Pot, add all ingredients except avocado and stir to combine.
2. Close the lid, select MANUAL, and cook at high pressure for 20 minutes.
3. When the cooking is complete, use a natural pressure release.
4. Remove the lid and with a slotted spoon, transfer the chicken breasts into a bowl.
5. With 2 forks, shred chicken breasts and then return to the pot. Mix to combine
6. Serve immediately with the topping of avocado pieces.

Nutritional Information (Per Serving)

Calories: 350
Fat: 25 g
Sat Fat: 10.8 g
Carbohydrates: 11.6 g
Fiber: 5.3 g
Sugar: 3.6 g
Protein: 20.9 g
Sodium: 316 mg

Turkey Chili

Yield: 8 servings
Preparation Time: 15 minutes
Cooking Time: 35 minutes
Total Time: 50 minutes
Ingredients:
1 tablespoon olive oil
1 red bell pepper, seeded and chopped
1 yellow onion, chopped
3 garlic cloves, minced
2 pounds ground turkey
2¼ cups tomatoes, chopped finely
1 (4-ounce) can fire-roasted diced green chilis
¾ cup homemade pumpkin puree
3 tablespoons red chili powder
1 tablespoon paprika
1 teaspoon cayenne pepper
1½ tablespoons ground cumin
1 tablespoon pumpkin pie spice
1 tablespoon dried oregano
Salt to taste
½ cup homemade chicken broth

Directions:

1. Place the oil in the Instant Pot and select SAUTÉ. Add the bell pepper, onion and garlic and cook for 4–5 minutes.

2. Ad turkey and cook for about 5 minutes.

3. Press CANCEL and stir in remaining ingredients.

4. Close the lid, select MANUAL, and cook at high pressure for 20 minutes.

5. When the cooking is complete, use a natural pressure release.

6. Serve hot.

Nutritional Information (Per Serving)
Calories: 346
Fat: 16.5 g
Sat Fat: 2.7 g
Carbohydrates: 22.7 g
Fiber: 8.5 g
Sugar: 11.5 g
Protein: 35.3 g
Sodium: 240 mg

Beef Chili

Yield: 6 servings
Preparation Time: 15 minutes
Cooking Time: 27 minutes
Total Time: 42 minutes
Ingredients:
1 tablespoon avocado oil
1 yellow onion, chopped
1 small red bell pepper, seeded and chopped
Salt to taste
4 garlic cloves, minced
2 tablespoons homemade tomato paste
2 pounds lean ground beef
3 tablespoons red chili powder
1 tablespoon ground cumin
1 tablespoon dried oregano, crushed
2 cups tomatoes, chopped
½ cup homemade chicken broth
2 tablespoons fresh lemon juice

Directions:
1. Place the oil in the Instant Pot and select SAUTÉ. Add the onion, bell pepper and a pinch of salt and cook for about 3 minutes.

2. Stir in garlic and tomato paste and cook for about 1 minute.

3. Add beef and salt and cook for 5–7 minutes.

4. Add spices and thyme and cook for about 1 minute.

5. Press CANCEL and stir in tomatoes and broth.

6. Close the lid, select MANUAL, and cook at high pressure for 15 minutes.

7. When the cooking is complete, use a natural pressure release.

8. Open the lid and stir in lemon juice.

9. Serve hot.

Nutritional Information (Per Serving)
Calories: 324
Fat: 14.9 g
Sat Fat: 6.3 g
Carbohydrates: 10.5 g
Fiber: 3.5 g
Sugar: 4.5 g
Protein: 33.2 g
Sodium: 241 mg

Beef & Pork Chili

Yield: 8 servings
Preparation Time: 15 minutes
Cooking Time: 35 minutes
Total Time: 50 minutes
Ingredients:
1 tablespoon olive oil
1 pound ground beef
1 pound ground pork
3 medium tomatillos, chopped
1 yellow onion, chopped
2 jalapeño peppers, chopped
2 garlic cloves, minced
6 ounces homemade tomato sauce
1 tablespoon red chili powder
1 tablespoon ground cumin
Salt and pepper to taste
¼ cup water

Directions:

1. Place the oil in the Instant Pot and select SAUTÉ. Then add the beef and pork and cook for about 5 minutes.

2. Remove extra grease from pot.

3. Press CANCEL and stir in remaining ingredients.

4. Close the lid, select MANUAL, and cook at high pressure for 35 minutes.

5. When the cooking is complete, use a natural pressure release.

6. Serve hot.

Nutritional Information (Per Serving)
Calories: 227
Fat: 10.6 g
Sat Fat: 2.9 g
Carbohydrates: 4.5 g
Fiber: 1.5 g
Sugar: 1.5 g
Protein: 7.2 g
Sodium: 257 mg

Beef Stew

Yield: 4 servings
Preparation Time: 15 minutes
Cooking Time: 35 minutes
Total Time: 50 minutes
Ingredients:
1¼ pounds beef chuck roast, cubed
Salt and pepper to taste
2 cups beef broth
¼ cup organic red wine
1½ tablespoons tomato paste
1 cup mushrooms, sliced
1 small yellow onion, diced
2 medium carrots, chopped
½ teaspoon dried thyme
½ teaspoon rosemary
1 bay leaf
2 cloves garlic, pressed
A handful fresh Italian parsley, chopped, to garnish

Directions:
1. Season beef with salt and pepper and place in the Instant Pot.
2. Whisk together beef broth, wine, and tomato paste in a bowl. Pour into the pot. Add rest of the ingredients and stir.
3. Close the lid. Select MEAT/STEW and cook at high pressure for 35 minutes.
4. Let the pressure release naturally.
5. Ladle into bowls. Garnish with parsley and serve.

Nutritional Information (Per Serving)
Calories: 593
Fat: 40.5 g

Sat Fat: 16 g

Carbohydrates: 10.9 g

Fiber: 2.4 g

Sugar: 5.7 g

Protein: 41.7 g

Mediterranean Vegetable Stew

Yield: 4 servings

Preparation Time: 15 minutes

Cooking Time: 5 minutes

Total Time: 20 minutes

Ingredients:

½ butternut squash, peeled, deseeded and cubed

1 cup zucchini, cubed

1 cup eggplant, cubed

5 ounces frozen okra, thawed

½ cup onions, chopped

1 small carrot, thinly sliced

3 tablespoons raisins

4 ounces canned tomato sauce

1 tomato, chopped

1 clove garlic, sliced

½ cup low sodium vegetable broth

A large pinch cinnamon powder

¼ teaspoon turmeric powder

Red chili flakes to taste

¼ teaspoon cumin powder

A large pinch paprika

Directions:

1. Add all the ingredients into the Instant Pot.

2. Close the lid, select MANUAL, and cook at high pressure for 5 minutes.

3. When the cooking is complete, do a quick pressure release.

4. Serve in soup bowls.

Nutritional Information (Per Serving)
Calories: 86
Fat: 0.4 g
Sat Fat: 0.1 g
Carbohydrates: 20.2 g
Fiber: 4.7 g
Sugar: 9.4 g
Protein: 2.7 g
Sodium: 216 mg

CHAPTER THREE

Poultry

Honey Chicken Thighs

Yield: 4 servings
Preparation Time: 15 minutes
Cooking Time: 21 minutes
Total Time: 36 minutes
Ingredients:
1 tablespoon olive oil
2 garlic cloves, minced
4 (4-ounce) skinless, boneless chicken thighs
Salt and pepper to taste
½ cup tomato sauce
¼ cup coconut aminos
2 tablespoons raw honey
2 tablespoons fresh lemon juice
1 tablespoon arrowroot starch
1 tablespoon water
2 tablespoons fresh basil, chopped

Directions:
1. Place the oil in the Instant Pot and select SAUTÉ. Add the garlic and cook for about 1 minute.

2. Add chicken thighs, salt and pepper and cook for about 5 minutes or until browned from all sides.

3. Press CANCEL and stir in tomato sauce, coconut aminos, honey and lemon juice.

4. Close the lid, select MANUAL, and cook at high pressure for 10 minutes.

5. When the cooking is complete, do a quick pressure release.

6. Meanwhile, in a small bowl, dissolve the arrowroot starch in water.

7. Open the lid and select SAUTÉ.

8. Stir in the arrowroot starch mixture. Cook for 4–5 minutes, stirring continuously.

9. Press CANCEL and serve hot with the garnishing of basil.

Nutritional Information (Per Serving)
Calories: 230
Fat: 7.6 g
Sat Fat: 2.1 g
Carbohydrates: 14.1 g
Fiber: 0.2 g
Sugar: 8 g
Protein: 25.5 g

Chicken with Olives

Yield: 8 servings
Preparation Time: 20 minutes
Cooking Time: 25 minutes
Total Time: 45 minutes
Ingredients:
1 teaspoon olive oil
3 pounds bone-in chicken leg quarters
1 pound cherry tomatoes, crushed slightly
2 garlic cloves, crushed
1 teaspoon dried oregano, crushed
¼ teaspoon red pepper flakes, crushed
Salt to taste
½ cup homemade chicken broth
½ cup green olives, pitted
1 tablespoon fresh basil leaves, torn

Directions:

1. Place the oil in the Instant Pot and select SAUTÉ. Add the chicken leg quarters and cook for 4–5 minutes.

2. With a slotted spoon, transfer the chicken leg quarters to a plate.

3. In the Instant Pot, add crushed cherry tomatoes with all juice, garlic, oregano, red pepper flakes and salt and cook for about 1 minute, scraping up the brown bits from bottom.

4. Press CANCEL and stir in the cooked chicken and broth.

5. Close the lid, select MANUAL, and cook at high pressure for 14 minutes.

6. When the cooking is complete, Press CANCEL and do a quick pressure release.

7. Open the lid and select SAUTÉ.

8. Stir in olives and basil and cook for about 2 minutes.

9. Press CANCEL and serve hot.

Nutritional Information (Per Serving)
Calories: 318
Fat: 21.5 g
Sat Fat: 5.6 g
Carbohydrates: 3.2 g
Fiber: 1.1 g
Sugar: 1.6 g
Protein: 29.8 g
Sodium: 417 mg

Cherry Tomato Chicken Cacciatore

Yield: 4 servings
Preparation Time: 10 minutes
Cooking Time: 20 minutes
Total Time: 30 minutes
Ingredients:
1½ pounds chicken thighs, bone-in
1 teaspoon olive oil
½ pound cherry tomatoes
½ cup water
Red pepper flakes to taste
½ teaspoon dried oregano
1 clove garlic, crushed
1 teaspoon salt
A sprig fresh basil, torn, to garnish
¼ cup green olives, pitted and rinsed, to garnish

Directions:
1. Place the tomatoes in a zip lock bag. Crush the tomatoes lightly with a meat mallet.

2. Select SAUTÉ and add oil. When the oil is heated, add chicken and cook until brown. Remove the chicken and set aside.

3. Add the crushed tomatoes, along with its juices into the Instant Pot. Add water, red pepper flakes, oregano, garlic and salt, and mix well. Scrape the bottom of the pot to remove any browned bits.

4. Add the cooked chicken and stir. Press CANCEL.

5. Close the lid, select MANUAL, and cook at high pressure for 13 minutes.

6. When the cooking is complete, do a quick pressure release.

7. Garnish with olives and basil and serve.

Nutritional Information (Per Serving)

Calories: 385
Fat: 27 g
Sat Fat: 7.7 g
Carbohydrates: 2.9 g
Fiber: 0.8 g
Sugar: 1.5 g
Protein: 30.7 g
Sodium: 753 mg

Buffalo Chicken

Yield: 6 servings
Preparation Time: 10 minutes
Cooking Time: 45 minutes
Total Time: 55 minutes
Ingredients:
2 pounds chicken breast
2 tablespoons coconut oil
2 onions, chopped
1 cup homemade chicken broth
1 pound sweet potatoes, peeled and cubed
6 tablespoons Paleo friendly buffalo sauce
1 teaspoon garlic powder
1 teaspoon onion powder
Salt and pepper to taste

Directions:
1. Select SAUTÉ and add the oil. When the oil is heated, add onions and sauté until brown.

2. Add the chicken, broth, sweet potatoes, buffalo sauce, salt, and all the spices into the pot. Mix well. Press CANCEL.

3. Close the lid, select MANUAL, and cook at high pressure for 15 minutes.

4. When the cooking is complete, do a quick pressure release.

Nutritional Information (Per Serving)
Calories: 333
Fat: 8.7 g
Sat Fat: 4 g
Carbohydrates: 26.6 g
Fiber: 4.6 g
Sugar: 2.3 g
Protein: 34.5 g

Herbed Whole Chicken

Yield: 6 servings
Preparation Time: 10 minutes
Cooking Time: 30 minutes
Total Time: 40 minutes
Ingredients:
1 tablespoon fresh rosemary, minced
½ tablespoon ground cumin
½ tablespoon cayenne pepper
½ tablespoon red pepper flakes, crushed
Salt and pepper to taste
1 4-pound roaster chicken
1½ cups homemade chicken broth

Directions:
1. In a bowl, mix together rosemary, salt, and spices. Rub the chicken with spice mixture generously.

2. Add the broth to the Instant Pot. Place a steamer rack in the pot and place the chicken over the rack.

3. Cook at high pressure for 25 minutes.

4. When the cooking is complete, do a quick pressure release.

5. Remove the lid and place chicken onto a cutting board for about 10 minutes before carving.

Nutritional Information (Per Serving)
Calories: 498
Fat: 10.8 g
Sat Fat: 3 g
Carbohydrates: 1.3 g
Fiber: 0.5 g
Sugar: 0.7 g
Protein: 92.3 g

Turkey Breast

Yield: 8 servings
Preparation Time: 15 minutes
Cooking Time: 55 minutes
Total Time: 1 hour 10 minutes
Ingredients:
1 cup homemade chicken broth
1 teaspoon dried rosemary, crushed
1 teaspoon dried parsley, crushed
1 teaspoon dried thyme crushed
1 teaspoon dried sage, crushed
1 teaspoon red pepper flakes, crushed
Salt and pepper to taste
1 (6 pounds) turkey breast

Directions:
1. In a bowl, mix together herbs, red pepper flakes, salt and pepper.
2. Rub turkey breast with the herb mixture generously.
3. At the bottom of Instant Pot, arrange a steamer trivet and pour 1½ cups of water.
4. Place the turkey breast on top of the trivet.
5. Press CANCEL. Close the lid and select POULTRY and the default setting.
6. When the cooking is complete, use a natural pressure release.
7. Preheat your broiler.
8. Open the lid and transfer turkey breast onto a baking sheet.
9. Broil for 5–10 minutes or until desired doneness.
10. Remove from oven and place the turkey breast on a cutting board to cool for 5–10 minutes.
11. Slice and serve.

Turkey Legs and Gravy

Yield: 4 servings
Preparation Time: 20 minutes
Cooking Time: 35 minutes
Total Time: 55 minutes
Ingredients:
4 (1-pound) turkey leg quarters
Salt and pepper to taste
2 tablespoons olive oil, divided
1 medium onion, chopped
3 garlic cloves, minced
1 large carrot, peeled and chopped
1 celery stalk, chopped
2 bay leaves
Pinch of dried rosemary
Pinch of dried thyme
Pinch of dried sage
1 tablespoon fresh lemon juice
1 cup homemade chicken broth
3 tablespoons arrowroot starch
2 tablespoons cold water

Directions:

1. Season the turkey quarters with salt and pepper generously.

2. Place 1 tablespoon of oil in the Instant Pot and select SAUTÉ. Add the turkey quarters and cook for 4–5 minutes per side.

3. Press CANCEL and transfer turkey quarters onto a plate.

4. Place remaining oil in the Instant Pot and select SAUTÉ. Add the onion and garlic and cook for about 1 minute.

5. Add carrot and celery and cook for 5–6 minutes.

6. Add bay leaves, herbs, salt and pepper and cook for about 1 minute.

7. Add lemon juice and scrape the brown bits.

8. Press CANCEL and stir in the turkey quarters and broth.

9. Close the lid, select MANUAL, and cook at high pressure for 20 minutes.

10. When the cooking is complete, do a natural pressure release for 10 minutes. Quick release the remaining pressure.

11. Open the lid and transfer the turkey quarters onto a platter.

12. In a small bowl, dissolve the arrowroot starch in water.

13. For gravy: select SAUTÉ and slowly, add the arrowroot starch mixture, stirring continuously.

14. Cook for 2–3 minutes or until desired thickness, stirring continuously.

15. Press CANCEL and transfer the gravy into a serving bowl.

16. Serve turkey quarters alongside the gravy.

Nutritional Information (Per Serving)
Calories: 767
Fat: 37.9 g
Sat Fat: 10.5 g
Carbohydrates: 10.8 g
Fiber: 1.4 g
Sugar: 2.4 g
Protein: 90 g
Sodium: 583 mg

Duck Legs

Yield: 4 servings
Preparation Time: 20 minutes
Cooking Time: 57 minutes
Total Time: 1 hour 17 minutes
Ingredients:
4 (7-ounce) duck legs
Salt and pepper to taste
½ tablespoon olive oil
¼ cup carrot, peeled and chopped
¼ cup celery stalk, chopped
¼ cup yellow onion, chopped
3 garlic cloves, chopped
1 cup homemade chicken broth
2 tablespoons fresh lemon juice
⅛ teaspoon dried sage
⅛ teaspoon dried thyme
2 tablespoons fresh parsley, chopped

Directions:
1. Season the duck legs with salt and pepper generously.

2. Place oil in the Instant Pot and select SAUTÉ. Add the duck legs and cook for about 5 minutes.

3. Press CANCEL and transfer duck legs onto a plate.

4. Remove grease from the pot, leaving about 1 teaspoon inside.

5. Select SAUTÉ and cook carrot, celery, onion and garlic for 1–2 minutes.

6. Press CANCEL and stir in the duck legs, broth, dried herbs, salt and pepper.

7. Close the lid, select MANUAL, and cook at high pressure for 20 minutes.

8. When the cooking is complete, Press CANCEL and do a quick pressure release.

9. Open the lid and with tongs, transfer the duck legs onto a platter.

10. With a hand blender, blend the onion mixture in the pot.

11. Select SAUTÉ and cook for 2–3 minutes.

12. Press CANCEL and transfer the gravy into a serving bowl.

13. Serve duck legs alongside gravy.

Nutritional Information (Per Serving)
Calories: 391
Fat: 14 g
Sat Fat: 3.1 g
Carbohydrates: 2.8 g
Fiber: 0.6 g
Sugar: 1.1 g
Protein: 59.4 g
Sodium: 457 mg

Roasted Quail

Yield: 2 servings
Preparation Time: 20 minutes
Cooking Time: 23 minutes
Total Time: 43 minutes
Ingredients:
2 (5-ounce) whole quails, cleaned and emptied and rinsed
Salt and pepper to taste
1 fresh thyme bunch
1 fresh rosemary bunch
½ cup homemade chicken broth
 3½ ounces bacon, chopped
1 small yellow onion, chopped finely
⅛ teaspoon dried rosemary
⅛ teaspoon dried thyme
1 bay leaf

Directions:
1. Season the quails with salt and black pepper slightly.
2. Stuff the cavity of quails with fresh herbs bunches.
3. Place the oil in the Instant Pot and select SAUTÉ. Add the bacon, onion, dried herbs, and bay leaf, and cook for about 3 minutes.
4. Place the quails in pot, breast-side down and cook for 4–5 minutes or until browned.
5. Flip the side and so that the quails are breast-side up.
6. Press CANCEL and add the broth in pot.
7. Close the lid, select MANUAL, and cook at high pressure for 7–9 minutes.
8. When the cooking is complete, do a quick pressure release.
9. With tongs, transfer quails onto a plate. Then, remove the herb sprigs from cavity.

10. Through a strainer, strain the cooking liquid into a bowl. Return the liquid to the pot and select SAUTÉ.

12. Cook for 3–4 minutes.

13. Add the quail and cook for about 2 minutes, pouring the sauce over quails occasionally.

14. Serve the quails with sauce.

Nutritional Information (Per Serving)
Calories: 320
Fat: 2.8 g
Sat Fat: 7.4 g
Carbohydrates: 4.3 g
Fiber: 0.8 g
Sugar: 1.7 g
Protein: 22.8 g
Sodium: 900 mg

CHAPTER FOUR

Meats

Beef Curry

Yield: 8 servings

Preparation Time: 15 minutes

Cooking Time: 45 minutes

Total Time: 60 minutes

Ingredients:

2 pounds beef stew meat

2 large onions, chopped

4 cloves garlic, chopped

Sea salt and pepper to taste

2 tablespoons mild curry powder

4 teaspoons fresh ginger, grated

3½ cups beef broth

1 cup fresh cilantro, chopped (optional)

2 tablespoons arrowroot powder mixed with 2–3 tablespoons water

Directions:

1. Add all the ingredients except arrowroot mixture and cilantro into the Instant Pot and stir.

2. Cover, select MEAT/STEW, and cook for 35 minutes.

3. When the cooking is complete, do a quick pressure release.

4. Open the lid, and set the Instant Pot to SAUTÉ.

5. Add the arrowroot mixture and stir constantly until thick.

6. Add cilantro and stir.

Nutritional Information (Per Serving)

Calories: 262
Fat: 8 g
Sat Fat: 2.9 g
Carbohydrates: 8 g
Fiber: 1.5 g
Sugar: 2 g
Protein: 37.4 g

Asian Style Short Ribs

Yield: 4 servings
Preparation Time: 10 minutes
Cooking Time: 45 minutes
Total Time: 55 minutes
Ingredients:
2 pounds beef short ribs
Lettuce cups to serve

For the sauce:
¼ cup coconut aminos
1 tablespoon apple cider vinegar
½ tablespoon ginger, grated
1 cup beef broth
2 tablespoons raw honey
3 cloves garlic, minced

To garnish:
½ tablespoon sesame oil, toasted
Sesame seeds, as required
1 green onion, thinly sliced.

Directions:
1. Place the short ribs in the Instant Pot.

2. Mix together all the ingredients of the sauce and add into the pot. Mix until well coated.

3. Cover, select MEAT/STEW, and cook for 45 minutes.

4. When the cooking is complete, do a quick pressure release.

5. Open the lid, and select SAUTÉ. Simmer until the cooking liquid thickens slightly. Press CANCEL.

6. Add sesame oil and stir.

7. Remove the meat and shred the meat. Pour sauce on top and serve garnished with sesame seeds and green onion. Serve over lettuce leaves.

Nutritional Information (Per Serving)
Calories: 546
Fat: 22.6 g
Sat Fat: 8.1 g
Carbohydrates: 13.8 g
Fiber: 0.4 g
Sugar: 9.1 g
Protein: 67.1 g
Sodium: 346 mg

Broccoli Beef

Yield: 3 servings
Preparation Time: 15 minutes
Cooking Time: 22 minutes
Total Time: 37 minutes
Ingredients:
1 pound flank steak, thinly sliced, chopped into strips
2 cups broccoli florets
1 cup low sodium beef broth
½ tablespoon sesame oil
¼ cup coconut aminos
½ tablespoon garlic, minced
¼ teaspoon ground ginger
¼ teaspoon red chili flakes or to taste
1 tablespoon arrowroot mixed with 2 tablespoons cold water
Salt to taste
Cooking spray

Directions:
1. Add all the ingredients except arrowroot mixture and broccoli into the Instant Pot.

2. Close the lid, select MANUAL, and cook at high pressure for 20 minutes.

3. When the cooking is complete, do a quick pressure release.

4. Open the lid, add broccoli.

5. Close the lid, select MANUAL, and cook at high pressure for 2 minutes.

6. When the cooking is complete, do a quick pressure release.

7. Add the arrowroot mixture. Mix well and serve.

Nutritional Information (Per Serving)
Calories: 372
Fat: 15.6 g

Sat Fat: 5.7 g
Carbohydrates: 9.4 g
Fiber: 1.7 g
Sugar: 1.3 g
Protein: 45.6 g

French Dip

Yield: 6 servings
Preparation Time: 10 minutes
Cooking Time: 45 minutes
Total Time: 55 minutes
Ingredients:
2 pounds beef chuck roast, trimmed of fat
4 cloves garlic
½ teaspoon pepper corns
Lettuce cups or Napa cabbage cups to serve
⅓ cup coconut aminos
¾ teaspoon dried rosemary
¾ teaspoon dried thyme
¾ teaspoon garlic powder
1½ cups water

Directions:
1. Add all the ingredients except lettuce cups to the Instant Pot.
2. Cover, select MEAT/STEW, and cook for 45 minutes.
3. When the cooking is complete, use a natural pressure release.
4. Remove the roast. When cool enough to handle, shred with a pair of forks.
5. Serve meat in lettuce cups, with cooking liquid served in cups or bowls to dip.

Italian Beef

Yield: 4 servings
Preparation Time: 15 minutes
Cooking Time: 45 minutes
Total Time: 60 minutes
Ingredients:
1 small onion, sliced
1 large carrot, chopped
1½ pounds beef roast, trimmed of fat
½ teaspoon dried oregano
2 cloves garlic, chopped
½ teaspoon garlic powder
½ teaspoon dried basil
¼ teaspoon dried thyme
Red chili flakes to taste
A large pinch ground cinnamon
¾ cup crushed tomatoes
½ tablespoon tomato paste
1 cup beef broth

Directions:
1. Add all the ingredients to the Instant Pot.
2. Cover, select MEAT/STEW, and cook for 45 minutes.

3. When the cooking is complete, use a natural pressure release.

4. Remove the roast. When cool enough to handle, shred with a pair of forks. Discard fat that is floating in the cooking liquid. Add beef back into the pot and stir.

Nutritional Information (Per Serving)
Calories: 367
Fat: 11.1 g
Sat Fat: 4.1 g
Carbohydrates: 9.1 g
Fiber: 2.9 g
Sugar: 4.8 g
Protein: 54.7 g
Sodium: 415 mg

Chuck Roast

Yield: 8 servings
Preparation Time: 15 minutes
Cooking Time: 1 hour 20 minutes
Total Time: 1 hour 35 minutes
Ingredients:
3 pounds beef chuck roast, trimmed and cut into large chunks
1 large yellow onion, sliced6 garlic cloves
2 (4-ounce) cans of green chilis
1 tablespoon dried oregano
Salt and pepper to taste
¼ cup fresh lime juice
¾ cup water

Directions:
1. In the Instant Pot, add all ingredients and stir to combine.
2. Close the lid, select MANUAL, and cook at high pressure for 1 hour.
3. When the cooking is complete, use a natural pressure release.
4. Open the lid and transfer the roast onto a plate.
5. With 2 forks, shred the meat and return to the Instant Pot.
6. Select SAUTÉ and cook for 15–20 minutes or until desired doneness of sauce.
7. Press CANCEL and serve hot.

Nutritional Information (Per Serving)
Calories: 639
Fat: 47 g
Sat Fat: 18.9 g
Carbohydrates: 4.3 g
Fiber: 0.6 g
Sugar: 1.8 g
Protein: 44.8 g

Flank Steak

Yield: 4 servings
Preparation Time: 15 minutes
Cooking Time: 23 minutes
Total Time: 38 minutes
Ingredients:
1 pound flank steaks, trimmed and cut into ¼-inch thick strips
Salt and pepper to taste
½ tablespoon olive oil
2 garlic cloves, minced
¼ cup water
¼ cup coconut aminos
2 tablespoons fresh lemon juice
1 tablespoon raw honey
1 tablespoon arrowroot starch
1½ tablespoons cold water
2 tablespoons fresh parsley, chopped

Directions:
1. Season the steak with salt and pepper evenly.
2. Place the oil in the Instant Pot and select SAUTÉ. Add the steak, salt and pepper and cook for about 5 minutes.
3. Transfer the beef to a bowl.
4. In the pot, add garlic and sauté for about 1 minute.
5. Press CANCEL and stir in beef, ¼ cup of water, coconut aminos, lemon juice and honey.
6. Close the lid, select MANUAL, and cook at high pressure for 12 minutes.
7. When the cooking is complete, do a quick pressure release.

8. Meanwhile, in a small bowl, dissolve the arrowroot starch in cold water.

9. Open the lid and select SAUTÉ.

10. Add the arrowroot mixture in Instant Pot, stirring continuously. Cook for 4–5 minutes or until desired thickness.

11. Press CANCEL and stir in parsley.

12. Serve hot.

Nutritional Information (Per Serving)
Calories: 278
Fat: 11.3 g
Sat Fat: 4.2 g
Carbohydrates: 9.9 g
Fiber: 0.2 g
Sugar: 4 g
Protein: 31.8 g
Sodium: 123 mg

Pork Shoulder

Yield: 4 servings
Preparation Time: 15 minutes
Cooking Time: 25 minutes
Total Time: 40 minutes
Ingredients:
1 small garlic clove, minced
¼ teaspoon dried rosemary, crushed
¼ teaspoon dried thyme, crushed
1 tablespoon olive oil
Salt and pepper to taste
1 pound boneless pork shoulder, trimmed and cubed
3 tablespoons water
2 tablespoons fresh lemon juice

Directions:

1. In a large bowl, add garlic, dried herbs, oil, salt and pepper and mix well.

2. Add pork and coat with garlic mixture generously. Keep aside for 15–20 minutes.

3. In the Instant Pot, place pork, water and lemon juice and stir to combine.

4. Close the lid, select MANUAL, and cook at high pressure for 25 minutes.

5. When the cooking is complete, use a natural pressure release.

6. Open the lid and with a slotted spoon, transfer pork to a large bowl.

7. With 2 forks, shred the meat.

8. Top with cooking liquid and serve.

Nutritional Information (Per Serving)
Calories: 196
Fat: 7.6 g
Sat Fat: 1.9 g
Carbohydrates: 0.5 g
Fiber: 0.1 g
Sugar: 0.2 g
Protein: 29.8 g
Sodium: 105 mg

Pork with Fruit

Yield: 5 servings
Preparation Time: 20 minutes
Cooking Time: 40 minutes
Total Time: 1 hour
Ingredients:
1⅓ pounds boneless pork tenderloin
2 cups apples, cored and chopped
2/3 cup fresh cherries, pitted
⅓ cup celery stalk, chopped
⅓ cup onion, chopped
½ cup fresh apple juice
Salt and pepper to taste

Directions:
1. In the Instant Pot, place all ingredients and stir to combine.
2. Close the lid and select MEAT and the default setting.
3. When the cooking is complete, use a natural pressure release.
4. Serve immediately.

Nutritional Information (Per Serving)
Calories: 209
Fat: 3.5 g
Sat Fat: 1.1 g
Carbohydrates: 21.5 g
Fiber: 3.1 g
Sugar: 17 g
Protein: 23.5 g
Sodium: 276 mg

Pulled Pork

Yield: 5 servings
Preparation Time: 10 minutes
Cooking Time: 30 minutes
Total Time: 40 minutes
Ingredients:
2 pounds pork loin
¼ cup chicken broth
½ teaspoon paprika or chili flakes or to taste
Salt and pepper to taste
¼ cup honey
1 teaspoon ground cumin
½ teaspoon chili powder
½ teaspoon garlic powder or 1 teaspoon garlic, minced
1 medium onion, chopped

Directions:
1. Add all the ingredients into the Instant Pot and stir.
2. Cover, select MEAT/STEW, and cook for 30 minutes.
3. When the cooking is complete, use a natural pressure release.
4. Remove the pork with a slotted spoon and place on your cutting board. When cool enough to handle, shred with a pair of forks.
5. Discard fat that is floating in the cooking liquid. Add pork back into the pot and stir.
6. Serve hot.

Nutritional Information (Per Serving)
Calories: 505
Fat: 25.5 g
Sat Fat: 9.5 g
Carbohydrates: 16.7 g
Fiber: 0.7 g

Sugar: 15 g
Protein: 50.3 g

Pork Chops with Mushroom Gravy

Yield: 6 servings
Preparation Time: 15 minutes
Cooking Time: 30 minutes
Total Time: 45 minutes
Ingredients:
6 pork chops, boneless, ¾ inch
1½ pounds mushrooms, sliced
½ tablespoon garlic, crushed
1 teaspoon dried rosemary
1 small onion, minced
A pinch pepper powder
Salt and pepper to taste
½ teaspoon paprika
1½ cups chicken broth
6 tablespoons lard or bacon fat, divided

Directions:
1. Select SAUTÉ. Add half the lard. When it melts, add the garlic and onion and stir-fry until the onion gets translucent.

2. Add the mushrooms and sauté until light brown. Cook in batches if necessary. Remove the mushrooms and set aside.

3. Add remaining lard into the pot. Sprinkle salt, pepper and paprika over the chops and add into the pot. Cook until brown on all the sides.

4. Add rest of the ingredients except the mushrooms and stir.

5. Close the lid, select MANUAL, and cook at high pressure for 15 minutes.

6. When the cooking is complete, use a natural pressure release.

7. Open the lid, add the mushrooms and stir. Select SAUTÉ, and simmer for 5–7 minutes.

8. Serve pork chops with the mushroom sauce.

Nutritional Information (Per Serving)
Calories: 503
Fat: 35.2 g
Sat Fat: 12.8 g
Carbohydrates: 16.1 g
Fiber: 4.6 g
Sugar: 8.3 g
Protein: 35.7 g

Honey, Pork and Apples

Yield: 4 servings
Preparation Time: 10 minutes
Cooking Time: 25 minutes
Total Time: 35 minutes
Ingredients:
2 pounds pork tenderloin, make few slits all over
¼ cup honey
1 large Granny Smith apples, cored and thinly sliced
1 tablespoon ground cinnamon
1 cup water
Salt to taste

Directions:
1. Place a slice or two of apple in the slits of the pork.

2. Place half the remaining apple slices at the bottom of the Instant Pot. Drizzle 2 tablespoons honey over the apples.

3. Place pork over the apples. Sprinkle with cinnamon and salt. Place remaining apple slices over the pork.

4. Add the water and drizzle 2 tablespoons honey over the apple slices on top.

5. Close the lid, select MANUAL, and cook at high pressure for 25 minutes.

6. When the cooking is complete, use a natural pressure release.

7. Slice the pork and serve with apples slices.

Nutritional Information (Per Serving)
Calories: 422
Fat: 8.1 g
Sat Fat: 2.7 g
Carbohydrates: 26.5 g
Fiber: 2.3 g
Sugar: 14.0 g
Protein: 23.2 g

Pork Carnitas

Yield: 3 servings
Preparation Time: 10 minutes
Cooking Time: 25 minutes
Total Time: 35 minutes
Ingredients:
1 pound pork loin, pat dried
2 cloves garlic, minced
1 small onion, chopped
1 small jalapeño, chopped
Juice of ½ navel orange
Juice of ½ lemon
1 teaspoon salt
1 cup water
Olive oil, to serve

For rub:
½ tablespoon dried oregano
½ tablespoon olive oil
1 teaspoon ground cumin
1 teaspoon pepper powder
½ teaspoon salt

Directions:
1. Mix together all the rub ingredients in a bowl. Rub pork with the mixture.

2. Place pork in the Instant Pot and place remaining ingredients on top.

3. Close the lid, select MANUAL, and cook at high pressure for 25 minutes.

4. When the cooking is complete, use a natural pressure release.

5. Remove pork and place on your cutting board. When cool enough to handle, shred the meat using forks.

6. To serve: Place a skillet over medium heat. Add a little olive oil. Swirl the pan so that the oil spreads. Spread Carnitas in the pan. Do not stir for a while. Cook until dry and the underside is crisp. Flip sides and cook the other side until light brown.

7. Serve with the cooking liquid drizzled on top.

Nutritional Information (Per Serving)
Calories: 405
Fat: 21.2 g
Sat Fat: 7.9 g
Carbohydrates: 9.9 g
Fiber: 2 g
Sugar: 5.4 g
Protein: 42.3 g
Sodium: 1258 mg

Roasted Leg of Lamb

Yield: 10 servings
Preparation Time: 15 minutes
Cooking Time: 1½ hours
Total Time: 1¾ hours
Ingredients:
1 (4-pound) bone-in leg of lamb
Salt and pepper to taste
1 tablespoon olive oil
1 large yellow onion, sliced thinly
1½ cups homemade chicken broth, divided
2 tablespoons fresh lemon juice
6 garlic cloves, crushed
6 fresh thyme sprigs
3 fresh rosemary sprigs

Directions:
1. Season the leg of lamb with salt and pepper generously.
2. Place the oil in the Instant Pot and select SAUTÉ. Add the leg of lamb and sear for about 4 minutes per side or until browned completely.
3. Transfer the leg of lamb to a large plate.
4. Add onion and a little salt to the pot and cook for about 5 minutes.
5. Add a little broth and cook for about 2 minutes, scraping the brown bits from bottom.
6. Press CANCEL and stir in the leg of lamb and remaining ingredients.
7. Close the lid, select MANUAL, and cook at high pressure for 75 minutes.
8. When the cooking is complete, use a natural pressure release.

9. Open the lid and with tongs, transfer the leg of lamb onto a cutting board.

10. Strain the pot liquid into a bowl.

11. Slice the leg of lamb and pour the strained pot liquid over.

12. Serve immediately.

Nutritional Information (Per Serving)
Calories: 315
Fat: 65 g
Sat Fat: 5 g
Carbohydrates: 2.2 g
Fiber: 0.6 g
Sugar: 9.8 g
Protein: 52 g
Sodium: 269 mg

Lamb with Bell Peppers

Yield: 8 servings
Preparation Time: 15 minutes
Cooking Time: 25 minutes
Total Time: 40 minutes
Ingredients:
1 tablespoon olive oil
2 onions, sliced thinly
4 garlic cloves, minced
¼ cup balsamic vinegar
2 pounds lamb shoulder, trimmed and cut into 2-inch cubes
2 cups tomatoes, chopped
2 bay leaves
1 teaspoon dried oregano, crushed
1 teaspoon dried basil, crushed
Salt and pepper to taste
1 large green bell pepper, seeded and cut into 8 slices

1 large red bell pepper, seeded and cut into 8 slices
¼ cup fresh parsley, chopped

Directions:

1. Place the oil in the Instant Pot and select SAUTÉ. Add the onion and garlic and cook for 2–3 minutes.

2. Add vinegar and scrape the brown bits from the bottom.

3. Press CANCEL and stir in lamb, tomatoes, bay leaves, herbs, salt and pepper.

4. Close the lid, select MANUAL, and cook at high pressure for 15 minutes.

5. When the cooking is complete, press CANCEL and use a natural pressure release.

6. Open the lid and select SAUTÉ.

7. Stir in bell peppers and cook for 4–5 minutes or until desired doneness.

8. Press CANCEL and stir in parsley.

9. Serve hot.

Nutritional Information (Per Serving)
Calories: 352
Fat: 13.8 g
Sat Fat: 4.3 g
Carbohydrates: 11.3 g
Fiber: 2.5 g
Sugar: 6.2 g
Protein: 44 g
Sodium: 150 mg

Lamb Shanks with Ginger and Figs

Yield: 3 servings
Preparation Time: 10 minutes
Cooking Time: 55 minutes
Total Time: 65 minutes
Ingredients:
1 tablespoon coconut oil
2 lamb shanks (12 ounces each)
1 medium onion, halved and thinly sliced
1 tablespoon fresh ginger, minced
1 tablespoon apple cider vinegar
2 cloves garlic, minced
5 dried figs, discard stems and halved lengthwise
1 tablespoon coconut aminos
1 teaspoon fish sauce
1 cup bone broth

Directions:
1. Select SAUTÉ and add oil. When the oil is heated, add lamb and cook until brown all over. Remove lamb with a slotted spoon and set aside.

2. Add onion and ginger and sauté until onions are translucent.

3. Add rest of the ingredients and stir. Scrape the bottom of the pot to remove any browned bits that are stuck.

4. Add the lamb and stir.

5. Close the lid, select MANUAL, and cook at high pressure for 20 minutes.

6. Let the pressure release naturally.

7. Discard the fat that is floating on the top. Serve lamb with the sauce.

Nutritional Information (Per Serving)
Calories: 444

Fat: 17.7 g
Sat Fat: 8.7 g
Carbohydrates: 39.4 g
Fiber: 6.8 g
Sugar: 20.9 g
Protein: 30.5 g
Sodium: 1031 mg

Spiced Pulled Lamb Shoulder

Yield: 6 servings
Preparation Time: 15 minutes
Cooking Time: 45 minutes
Total Time: 60 minutes
Ingredients:
3 pounds lamb shoulder, cut into smaller pieces to fit in the Instant Pot
2 onions, quartered
1 tablespoon paprika
1 tablespoon sumac
1½ teaspoons chili powder or to taste
2 tablespoons ground cumin
1 tablespoon ground cinnamon
1½ teaspoons garlic, minced
1 tablespoon ginger, grated
Lemon juice, as required
5 tablespoons olive oil
Salt and pepper to taste
1 cup water
A handful fresh parsley, chopped to garnish

Directions:
1. Add all the spices, salt, and oil and lemon juice into a bowl and mix well.

2. Score the lamb at different places. Rub the spice mixture all over the lamb. Place lamb in the Instant Pot.

3. Add water and place onions over the lamb.

4. Cover and select MEAT/STEW for 45 minutes.

5. When the cooking is complete, use a natural pressure release.

6. Remove the lamb pieces from the pot. When cool enough to handle, shred the lamb and add it back to the pot.

7. Taste and adjust the seasonings. Cover and heat thoroughly. Garnish with parsley and serve.

Nutritional Information (Per Serving)
Calories: 564
Fat: 29.4 g
Sat Fat: 7.8 g
Carbohydrates: 8.7 g
Fiber: 3 g
Sugar: 2.9 g
Protein: 65.1 g

Lamb Curry

Yield: 3 servings
Preparation Time: 15 minutes
Cooking Time: 35 minutes
Total Time: 50 minutes
Ingredients:
¾ pound lamb stew meat
1 tablespoon ginger, minced
2 cloves garlic, minced
1 cup coconut milk
7 ounces canned diced tomatoes
Juice of a lime
3 small carrots, chopped

1 small zucchini, chopped
1 small onion, chopped
¾ teaspoon garam masala
2 tablespoons ground coriander
½ teaspoon turmeric
1 teaspoon chili powder
A handful fresh cilantro, chopped
2 tablespoons ghee
Salt and pepper to taste
½ cup water

Directions:

1. Add garlic, ginger, salt, pepper, lime juice and coconut milk into a large bowl and mix well. Cover and refrigerate for 1–4 hours.

2. Select SAUTÉ. Add ghee. When ghee melts, add onions and sauté until golden brown. Add meat and the chilled mixture.

3. Add tomatoes and sauté for 2 minutes. Add rest of the ingredients and stir. Press CANCEL button.

4. Cover, select MEAT/STEW, cook for 35 minutes.

5. When the cooking is complete, use a natural pressure release.

6. Garnish with cilantro and serve with cauliflower rice.

Nutritional Information (Per Serving)
Calories: 535
Fat: 36.4 g
Sat Fat: 25.3 g
Carbohydrates: 19.3 g
Fiber: 5.5 g
Sugar: 9 g
Protein: 35.9 g

CHAPTER FIVE

Seafood

Salmon with Veggies

Yield: 4 servings
Preparation Time: 20 minutes
Cooking Time: 6 minutes
Total Time: 26 minutes
Ingredients:
1 pound skin-on salmon fillets
Salt and pepper to taste
1 parsley sprig
1 dill sprig
3 teaspoons coconut oil, melted and divided
½ lemon, sliced thinly
1 carrot, peeled and julienned
1 zucchini, peeled and julienned
1 red bell pepper, seeded and julienned

Directions:
1. Season the salmon fillets with salt and pepper evenly.

2. At the bottom of Instant Pot, arrange a steamer trivet and place herb sprigs and 1 cup of water.

3. Place the salmon fillets on top of the trivet, skin side down.

4. Drizzle salmon fillets with 2 teaspoons of coconut oil and top with lemon slices.

5. Close the lid, select STEAM and cook for 3 minutes.

6. When the cooking is complete, use a natural pressure release.

7. Meanwhile, for sauce: in a bowl, add remaining ingredients and mix until well combined.

8. Open the lid and transfer the salmon fillets onto a platter.

9. Remove the steamer trivet, herbs and cooking water from pot. With paper towels, pat dry the pot.

10. Place the remaining coconut oil in the Instant Pot and select SAUTÉ. Then add the veggies and cook or 2–3 minutes.

11. Press CANCEL and transfer the veggies onto the platter with salmon.

12. Serve immediately.

Nutritional Information (Per Serving)
Calories: 204
Fat: 10.6 g
Sat Fat: 4 g
Carbohydrates: 5.7 g
Fiber: 1.4 g
Sugar: 3.2 g
Protein: 23.1 g
Sodium: 105 mg

Spiced Salmon

Yield: 4 servings
Preparation Time: 15 minutes
Cooking Time: 5 minutes
Total Time: 20 minutes
Ingredients:
4 (5-ounce) salmon fillets
Salt and pepper to taste
2 jalapeño peppers, seeded and chopped finely
3 garlic cloves, minced
2 tablespoons fresh parsley, chopped
3 tablespoons fresh lime juice
2 tablespoons olive oil
2 tablespoons raw honey
2 tablespoons hot water
1 teaspoon ground cumin
1 teaspoon paprika

Directions:
1. Season the salmon fillets with salt and pepper evenly.

2. For sauce: in a bowl, add remaining ingredients and mix until well combined.

3. At the bottom of Instant Pot, arrange a steamer trivet and pour 1 cup of water.

4. Place the salmon fillets on top of the trivet.

5. Close the lid, select STEAM and cook for 5 minutes.

6. When the cooking is complete, do a quick pressure release.

7. Transfer the salmon onto a serving plate.

8. Drizzle with sauce and serve.

Nutritional Information (Per Serving)
Calories: 290
Fat: 16.1 g

Sat Fat: 2.3 g
Carbohydrates: 10.6 g
Fiber: 0.7 g
Sugar: 9 g
Protein: 28 g
Sodium: 288 mg

Cod Parcel

Yield: 6 servings
Preparation Time: 15 minutes
Cooking Time: 5 minutes
Total Time: 20 minutes
Ingredients:
2 (4-ounce) cod fillets
½ teaspoon garlic powder
Salt and pepper to taste
2 fresh dill sprigs
4 lemon slices
2 tablespoons olive oil

Directions:
1. Arrange 2 large parchment squares onto a smooth surface.
2. Place 1 fillet in the center of each parchment square and sprinkle with garlic powder, salt and pepper.
3. Top each fillet with 1 dill sprig, 2 lemon slices and 1 tablespoon of oil.
4. Fold each parchment paper around the fillets to seal.
5. At the bottom of Instant Pot, arrange a steamer trivet and pour 1 cup of water.
6. Place the fish parcels on top of the trivet in a single layer.
7. Close the lid, choose MANUAL, and cook at low pressure for 5 minutes.
8. When the cooking is complete, do a quick pressure release.

9. Open the lid and transfer the fish parcels onto serving plates.

10. Unwrap the parcels and serve.

Nutritional Information (Per Serving)
Calories: 215
Fat: 15 g
Sat Fat: 2 g
Carbohydrates: 1 g
Fiber: 0.2 g
Sugar: 0.3 g
Protein: 20.4 g
Sodium: 149 mg

Maple Glazed Cod

Yield: 4 servings
Preparation Time: 15 minutes
Cooking Time: 5 minutes
Total Time: 20 minutes
Ingredients:
4 (4-ounce) cod fillets
Salt and pepper to taste
6 garlic cloves, minced
⅓ cup fresh lemon juice
¼ cup maple syrup
1 tablespoon coconut aminos
½ teaspoon red pepper flakes

Directions:
1. Season cod with salt and pepper evenly.

2. In a bowl, mix together remaining ingredients.

3. At the bottom of Instant Pot, arrange a steamer trivet and pour 1 cup of water.

4. Place the cod fillets on top of the trivet in a single layer and top with sauce.

5. Close the lid, select STEAM and cook for 5 minutes.

6. When the cooking is complete, use a natural pressure release.

7. Serve hot.

Nutritional Information (Per Serving)
Calories: 159
Fat: 1.3 g
Sat Fat: 0.2 g
Carbohydrates: 16 g
Fiber: 0.2 g
Sugar: 12.2 g
Protein: 0.7 g
Sodium: 121 mg

Shrimp in Wine Sauce

Yield: 4 servings
Preparation Time: 15 minutes
Cooking Time: 5 minutes
Total Time: 20 minutes
Ingredients:
2 tablespoons olive oil
2 shallots, chopped
1 tablespoon garlic, crushed
¼ cup white wine
1 pound frozen large shrimp, peeled and deveined
½ cup homemade chicken broth
2 tablespoons fresh lemon juice
Salt and pepper to taste

Directions:

1. Place the oil in the Instant Pot and select SAUTÉ. Add the shallots and cook for about 2 minutes.

2. Add the garlic and sauté for about 1 minute.

3. Stir in the wine and cook for about 1 minute.

4. Press CANCEL and stir in the shrimp, broth, lemon juice, salt and pepper.

5. Close the lid, select MANUAL, and cook at high pressure for 1 minute.

6. When the cooking is complete, do a quick pressure release.

7. Serve hot.

Nutritional Information (Per Serving)
Calories: 223
Fat: 9.2 g
Sat Fat: 1.7 g
Carbohydrates: 4.6 g
Fiber: o.1 g
Sugar: 0.4 g
Protein: 26.9 g
Sodium: 331 mg

Shrimp Creole

Yield: 4 servings
Preparation Time: 15 minutes
Cooking Time: 5 minutes
Total Time: 20 minutes
Ingredients:

2 pounds medium shrimp, deveined and shelled

2½ cups onions, finely diced

2 cups bell pepper, chopped

2 cans (28 ounces each) whole tomatoes, crushed

2 cans (8 ounce each) tomato sauce

2 cloves garlic, minced

3 cups celery, chopped

1 teaspoon creole seasoning or to taste

Salt to taste

Freshly ground pepper to taste

1–2 tablespoons Tabasco sauce or any other hot sauce or to taste

Directions:

1. Add all the ingredients into the Instant Pot.

2. Close the lid, choose MANUAL, and cook at low pressure for 5 minutes.

3. When the cooking is complete, do a quick pressure release.

Nutritional Information (Per Serving)
Calories: 376
Fat: 3.8 g
Sat Fat: 0.2 g
Carbohydrates: 36 g
Fiber: 9.1 g
Sugar: 21 g
Protein: 55.4 g

Curry Shrimp

Yield: 6 servings
Preparation Time: 10 minutes
Cooking Time: 5 minutes
Total Time: 15 minutes
Ingredients:
1½ pounds shrimp, with shells
2½ cups water
¾ cup Thai red curry sauce or 2–3 tablespoons red curry paste
5½ cups light coconut milk
4 teaspoons lemon garlic seasoning
⅓ cup cilantro, chopped

Directions:
1. Add all the ingredients except cilantro into the Instant Pot. Mix until well combined.

2. Close the lid, choose MANUAL, and cook at low pressure for 5 minutes.

3. When the cooking is complete, do a quick pressure release.

4. Sprinkle cilantro on top and serve.

Nutritional Information (Per Serving)
Calories: 648
Fat: 54.5 g
Sat Fat: 47.1 g
Carbohydrates: 15.4 g
Fiber: 4.9 g
Sugar: 7.9 g
Protein: 30.9 g
Sodium: 552 mg

Lemony Mussels

Yield: 4 servings
Preparation Time: 15 minutes
Cooking Time: 7 minutes
Total Time: 23 minutes
Ingredients:
1 tablespoon olive oil
1 medium yellow onion, chopped
1 garlic clove, minced
½ teaspoon dried rosemary, crushed
1 cup homemade chicken broth
2 tablespoons fresh lemon juice
Salt and pepper to taste
2 pounds mussels, cleaned and de-bearded

Directions:
1. Place the oil in the Instant Pot and select SAUTÉ. Add the onion and cook for about 5 minutes.

2. Add garlic and rosemary and cook for about 1 minute.

3. Press CANCEL and stir in the broth, lemon juice and pepper.

4. Arrange a steamer trivet on top of broth mixture.

5. Place the mussels on top of the trivet.

6. Close the lid, select MANUAL, and cook at low pressure for 1 minute.

7. When the cooking is complete, do a quick pressure release.

8. Transfer the mussels to serving bowls.

9. Top with the cooking liquid and serve.

Nutritional Information (Per Serving)
Calories: 249
Fat: 9 g
Sat Fat: 1.6 g
Carbohydrates: 11.7 g

Fiber: 0.7 g

Sugar: 1.5 g

Protein: 28.6 g

Sodium: 880 mg

Moroccan Fish Tagine

Yield: 6 servings

Preparation Time: 15 minutes

Cooking Time: 10 minutes

Total Time: 25 minutes

Ingredients:

2/3 cup extra-virgin olive oil

2 onions, halved and thinly sliced

6 tablespoons tomato paste

2 teaspoons garam masala

½ teaspoon cayenne pepper

4 tomatoes, chopped

1 cup kalamata olives, pitted and coarsely chopped

3 pounds cod fillets, 1 inch thick, cut into 2 inch pieces

4 fennel bulbs, retain ½ cup fennel fronds and mince them, slice the bulbs into ¼ inch thick slices

Salt and pepper to taste

8 cloves garlic, minced

3 teaspoons paprika

4 cups homemade chicken broth

4 strips (2 inches each) lemon zest

½ cup raisins

¼ cup fresh parsley, chopped

Directions:

1. Select SAUTÉ. Add half the oil. When the oil is heated, add fennel bulb, onion and about ½ teaspoons salt and sauté until light brown.

2. Add garlic, tomato paste and spices and sauté until fragrant. Add broth and mix well. Scrape the bottom of the pot to remove any browned bits that are stuck. Press CANCEL.

3. Add tomatoes, lemon zest, olives and raisins, and stir.

4. Place the fish into a steamer basket and close the lid. Cook at high pressure for 5 minutes.

5. When the cooking is complete, do a quick pressure release. Discard lemon zest.

6. Serve cod in individual serving plates. Garnish with parsley and fennel fronds. Drizzle remaining half olive oil and serve.

Nutritional Information (Per Serving)
Calories: 561
Fat: 28.6 g
Sat Fat: 3.9 g
Carbohydrates: 34.7 g
Fiber: 9 g
Sugar: 13.5 g
Protein: 48 g

Seafood Cioppino

Yield: 3 servings
Preparation Time: 15 minutes
Cooking Time: 10 minutes
Total Time: 25 minutes
Ingredients:
¾ pound fish fillets like cod, halibut, haddock, or mahi mahi, cut into 1 inch pieces
½ pound mussels
¼ pound raw shrimp, peeled and deveined

½ pound clams

4 ounces clam juice

1 tablespoon lard or bacon fat

1 small onion, chopped

1 medium shallot, chopped

2 cloves garlic, minced

2 ribs celery, chopped (optional)

3 ounces canned tomato paste

1 large tomato, diced

3 cups chicken broth

1½ teaspoons Italian seasoning

1 bay leaf

A handful fresh parsley, chopped

Sea salt and pepper to taste

¼ teaspoon crushed red pepper

Directions:

1. Select SAUTÉ. Add lard. When it melts, add the garlic and onion and stir fry until translucent. Press CANCEL.

2. Add all the ingredients except parsley to the Instant Pot.

3. Close the lid, choose MANUAL, and cook at low pressure for 5 minutes.

4. When the cooking is complete, do a quick pressure release.

5. Discard the bay leaf. Add parsley. Mix well and serve.

Nutritional Information (Per Serving)
Calories: 395
Fat: 11.2 g
Sat Fat: 3 g
Carbohydrates: 25.5 g
Fiber: 3.3 g
Sugar: 10.4 g
Protein: 47.2 g

Fish and Tomatoes

Yield: 6 servings
Preparation Time: 15 minutes
Cooking Time: 5 minutes
Total Time: 20 minutes
Ingredients:
3 pounds cod
1 large onion, sliced
1½ cans (15 ounces each) diced tomatoes
⅓ cup low sodium broth
Salt, pepper and red pepper flakes to taste
1 large bell pepper, sliced
5 cloves garlic, minced
1½ tablespoons rosemary
Seasoning of your choice, as required

Directions:
1. Set aside the fish and seasoning and add rest of the ingredients into the Instant Pot. Mix well.
2. Sprinkle seasoning all over the fish as well as on the mixture. Place fish on the mixture.
3. Close the lid, select MANUAL, and cook at high pressure for 5 minutes.
4. When the cooking is complete, do a quick pressure release.

Nutritional Information (Per Serving)
Calories: 277
Fat: 2.4 g
Sat Fat: 0.5 g
Carbohydrates: 8.8 g
Fiber: 2.3 g
Sugar: 4.5 g
Protein: 53.1 g

CHAPTER SIX

Vegetables

Zucchini with Tomatoes

Yield: 8 servings
Preparation Time: 15 minutes
Cooking Time: 11 minutes
Total Time: 26 minutes
Ingredients:
1 tablespoon olive oil
2 small yellow onions, chopped roughly
2 garlic cloves, minced
6 medium zucchinis, chopped roughly
1 pound cherry tomatoes
1 cup water
Salt and pepper to taste
2 tablespoons fresh basil, chopped

Directions:
1. Place the oil in the Instant Pot and select SAUTÉ. Add the onion and garlic and cook for 3–4 minutes.

2. Add zucchinis and tomatoes and cook for 1–2 minutes.

3. Press CANCEL and stir in remaining ingredients except basil.

4. Close the lid, select MANUAL, and cook at high pressure for 5 minutes.

5. When the cooking is complete, use a natural pressure release.

6. Remove the lid and transfer the vegetable mixture onto a serving platter.

7. Garnish with basil and serve.

Nutritional Information (Per Serving)
Calories: 57
Fat: 2.1 g
Sat Fat: 12 g
Carbohydrates: 9 g
Fiber: 2.7 g
Sugar: 4.8 g
Protein: 2.5 g
Sodium: 38 mg

Mixed Veggies

Yield: 4 servings
Preparation Time: 20 minutes
Cooking Time: 7 minutes
Total Time: 27 minutes
Ingredients:
1 large zucchini, sliced into thin circles
1 medium eggplant, sliced into thin circles
2 medium tomatoes, sliced into thin circles
1 small red onion, sliced into thin circles
1 tablespoon fresh thyme leaves, minced and divided
Salt and pepper to taste
2 large garlic cloves, minced
2 tablespoons olive oil
1 tablespoon balsamic vinegar

Directions:
1. In a bowl, add all vegetables, half of thyme, salt and pepper and toss to coat well.

2. At the bottom of a foil lined springform, spread some of garlic.

3. Arrange alternating slices of zucchini, eggplant, tomatoes and onion, starting at the outer edge of the pan towards the center, overlapping the slices slightly.

4. Sprinkle with the remaining garlic, thyme, salt and pepper. Drizzle with oil and vinegar evenly.

5. At the bottom of Instant Pot, arrange a steamer trivet and pour 1 cup of water.

6. Place the springform pan on top of trivet.

7. Close the lid, select MANUAL, and cook at high pressure for 6 minutes.

8. When the cooking is complete, do a natural pressure release for 5 minutes. Quick release the remaining pressure.

9. Serve hot.

Nutritional Information (Per Serving)
Calories: 125
Fat: 7.6 g
Sat Fat: 1.1 g
Carbohydrates: 14.4 g
Fiber: 6.3 g
Sugar: 7.3 g
Protein: 3 g
Sodium: 54 mg

Vegetable Korma

Yield: 5 servings
Preparation Time: 15 minutes
Cooking Time: 3 minutes
Total Time: 18 minutes
Ingredients:
1 medium cauliflower, cut into florets
¾ cup green beans, trimmed and cut into 2 inch pieces
1 clove garlic, minced
1 large carrot, chopped into chunks
1 medium onion, chopped
1 cup coconut milk
1 teaspoons sea salt or to taste
1 tablespoon curry powder
½ teaspoon garam masala
1 tablespoon arrowroot powder mixed with 2 tablespoons water
½ tablespoon red pepper flakes (optional)

Directions:
1. Set aside the vegetables, and add all the ingredients except arrowroot mixture into the Instant Pot. Mix well.
2. Add all the vegetables and mix well.
3. Close the lid, select MANUAL, and cook at high pressure for 3 minutes.
4. When the cooking is complete, do a quick pressure release.
5. Add the arrowroot mixture. Mix well and serve over cauliflower rice.

Nutritional Information (Per Serving)
Calories: 173
Fat: 11.9 g
Sat Fat: 10.2 g
Carbohydrates: 16.2 g

Fiber: 5.9 g
Sugar: 6.3 g
Protein: 4.3 g
Sodium: 429 mg

Thai Spaghetti Squash Curry

Yield: 4 servings
Preparation Time: 10 minutes
Cooking Time: 8 minutes
Total Time: 18 minutes
Ingredients:
2 pounds spaghetti squash, halved and deseeded
1 tablespoon Thai red curry paste
½ cup coconut milk
½ cup water
4 cloves garlic, minced
1 tablespoon cilantro

Directions:
1. Prick some holes on the top of the spaghetti squash with a fork.

2. Add coconut milk, curry paste, garlic and water into the Instant Pot. Mix well.

3. Place the squash in the pot with its cut side down.

4. Close the lid, select MANUAL, and cook at high pressure for 8 minutes.

5. When the cooking is complete, use a natural pressure release.

6. Scoop out the squash into a bowl and mash it. Transfer it back to the pot. Mix until well blended with the coconut milk mixture.

7. Sprinkle cilantro on top and serve.

Nutritional Information (Per Serving)
Calories: 159
Fat: 9.6 g
Sat Fat: 7 g
Carbohydrates: 19.1 g
Fiber: 0.7 g
Sugar: 1 g
Protein: 2.3 g
Sodium: 240 mg

Pumpkin Curry

Yield: 4 servings
Preparation Time: 15 minutes
Cooking Time: 8 minutes
Total Time: 23 minutes
Ingredients:
1 tablespoon coconut oil
1 small onion, chopped
½ tablespoon garlic, minced
½ tablespoon fresh ginger, minced
1 serrano pepper, halved
½ teaspoon cumin seeds
4 cups pumpkin, peeled and chopped
1 tomato, chopped
2 teaspoons ground coriander
¼ teaspoon red chili powder
¼ teaspoon ground turmeric
Salt to taste
¼ cup water

Directions:

1. Place the coconut oil in the Instant Pot and select SAUTÉ. Add the onion, garlic, ginger, serrano pepper and cumin and cook for 2–3 minutes.

2. Press CANCEL and stir in remaining ingredients.

3. Close the lid, select MANUAL, and cook at high pressure for 5 minutes.

4. When the cooking is complete, do a quick pressure release.

5. Serve hot.

Nutritional Information (Per Serving)
Calories: 129
Fat: 4.3 g
Sat Fat: 12 g
Carbohydrates: 23.3 g
Fiber: 8 g
Sugar: 9 g
Protein: 3.3 g
Sodium: 55 mg

Greens Curry

Yield: 4 servings
Preparation Time: 15 minutes
Cooking Time: 20 minutes
Total Time: 35 minutes
Ingredients:
2 tablespoons coconut oil
1 medium onion, chopped
4 garlic cloves, minced
1 teaspoon fresh ginger, minced
1 teaspoon ground cumin
1 teaspoon ground coriander
½ teaspoon red chili powder
½ teaspoon ground turmeric
Salt and pepper to taste
1 pound fresh mustard greens, rinsed
1 pound fresh spinach, rinsed

Directions:
1. Place the coconut oil in the Instant Pot and select SAUTÉ. Add the onion, garlic, ginger and spices and cook for 2–3 minutes.

2. Add the greens and cook for about 2 minutes.

3. Press CANCEL and stir well.

4. Close the lid, select MANUAL, and cook at high pressure for 4 minutes.

5. When the cooking is complete, use a natural pressure release.

6. Open the lid and with a hand blender, blend the mixture until smooth.

7. Serve immediately.

Nutritional Information (Per Serving)
Calories: 135

Fat: 7.8 g
Sat Fat: 6 g
Carbohydrates: 14.2 g
Fiber: 7.2 g
Sugar: 3.6 g
Protein: 7 g
Sodium: 163 mg

Veggies Curry

Yield: 8 servings
Preparation Time: 20 minutes
Cooking Time: 10 minutes
Total Time: 30 minutes
Ingredients:
2 tablespoons olive oil
2 teaspoons garlic, minced
1½ pounds sweet potatoes, peeled and chopped
1 pound fresh mushrooms, quartered
2 cups unsweetened coconut milk
2 tablespoons coconut aminos
1 teaspoon dried basil
½ teaspoon ground coriander
¼ teaspoon ground cardamom
⅛ teaspoon ground cinnamon
Pinch of red pepper flakes
Salt to taste
2 medium bunches broccoli, cut into small florets
2 tablespoons fresh lime juice

Directions:
1. Place the oil in the Instant Pot and select SAUTÉ. Add the garlic and cook for about 1 minute.

2. Add sweet potato and mushrooms and cook for 2–3 minutes.

3. Press CANCEL and stir in remaining ingredients except broccoli and lime juice.

4. Close the lid, select MANUAL, and cook at high pressure for 3 minutes.

5. When the cooking is complete, do a quick pressure release.

6. Open the lid and stir in the broccoli florets.

7. Close the lid, select MANUAL, and cook at low pressure for 2–3 minutes.

8. When the cooking is complete, do a quick pressure release.

9. Open the lid and stir in lime juice.

10. Serve hot.

Nutritional Information (Per Serving)
Calories: 328
Fat: 18.5 g
Sat Fat: 13.2 g
Carbohydrates: 38.3 g
Fiber: 8.7 g
Sugar: 5.5 g
Protein: 8 g

Mashed Sweet Potatoes

Yield: 4 servings
Preparation Time: 15 minutes
Cooking Time: 10 minutes
Total Time: 25 minutes
Ingredients:
For mash:
½ cup apple juice, unsweetened, divided
1 pound sweet potatoes, peeled and cut into ½ inch thick slices
½ tablespoon ground cinnamon

½ teaspoon all spice

½ teaspoon ground nutmeg

½ cup water

A large pinch ground cloves

For topping:

A pinch cinnamon

A pinch nutmeg

¼ cup apple juice

2 tablespoons pecans

Maple syrup to taste (optional)

Directions:

1. Add all the ingredients of the mash (retain ¼ cup apple juice) into the Instant Pot.

2. Close the lid, select MANUAL, and cook at high pressure for 10 minutes.

3. When the cooking is complete, do a quick pressure release.

4. Mash the sweet potatoes along with remaining apple juice.

5. Add the ingredients of the topping except the pecans. Mix well.

6. Sprinkle pecans on top and serve warm.

Nutritional Information (Per Serving)
Calories: 209
Fat: 5.4 g
Sat Fat: 0.6 g
Carbohydrates: 39 g
Fiber: 6.1 g
Sugar: 5.6 g
Protein: 2.6 g
Sodium: 49 mg

Braised Kale and Carrots

Yield: 4 servings
Preparation Time: 15 minutes
Cooking Time: 10 minutes
Total Time: 25 minutes
Ingredients:
20 ounces kale, discard hard stems and ribs, chopped
2 teaspoons ghee
6 carrots, cut into ½ inch slices
2 medium onions, thinly sliced
Salt and pepper to taste
1 cup vegetable broth
2 teaspoons balsamic vinegar
½ teaspoon red pepper flakes

Directions:
1. Select SAUTÉ. Add ghee. When it melts, add onions and carrots and sauté until translucent. Press CANCEL.
2. Add rest of the ingredients. Mix well.
3. Close the lid, select MANUAL, and cook at high pressure for 4 minutes.
4. When the cooking is complete, do a quick pressure release.

Nutritional Information (Per Serving)
Calories: 159
Fat: 2.6 g
Sat Fat: 1.4 g
Carbohydrates: 29.3 g
Fiber: 5.6 g
Sugar: 7 g
Protein: 6.8 g

Glazed Carrots

Yield: 4 servings
Preparation Time: 15 minutes
Cooking Time: 3 minutes
Total Time: 18 minutes
Ingredients:
1 pound carrots
2 tablespoons olive oil
2 tablespoons raw honey
2 tablespoons Dijon mustard
2 teaspoons garlic, minced
1 teaspoon ground cumin
½ teaspoon paprika
Salt and pepper to taste

Directions:
1. Cut the carrots into quarters lengthwise and then cut each quarter in half.

2. At the bottom of Instant Pot, arrange a steamer trivet and pour 1 cup of water.

3. Place the carrots on top of the trivet.

4. Close the lid, select MANUAL, and cook at high pressure for 2 minutes.

5. When the cooking is complete, do a quick pressure release.

6. Open the lid and transfer the carrots onto a plate.

7. Remove water from the pot and with paper towels, pat dry it.

8. Place the oil in the Instant Pot and select SAUTÉ. Add the remaining ingredients and cook for about 1 minute.

9.Stir in the carrots and cook for about 1 minute.

10. Press CANCEL and serve warm.

Nutritional Information (Per Serving)

Calories: 148
Fat: 7.5 g
Sat Fat: 1 g
Carbohydrates: 21.1 g
Fiber: 3.3 g
Sugar: 14.3 g
Protein: 1.5 g
Sodium: 207 mg

Instant Pot Root Vegetables

Yield: 2 servings
Preparation Time: 15 minutes
Cooking Time: 8 minutes
Total Time: 23 minutes
Ingredients:
1 sweet potato, peeled and cubed

1 parsnip, cubed

2 carrots, cubed

1 red onion, sliced

1 cup vegetable broth

2 teaspoons coconut oil

½ teaspoon oregano

½ teaspoon dried basil

Directions:
1. Add all the ingredients into the Instant Pot and stir.

2. Close the lid, select MANUAL, and cook at high pressure for 8 minutes.

3. When the cooking is complete, do a quick pressure release.

Nutritional Information (Per Serving)
Calories: 208
Fat: 5.6 g
Sat Fat: 4.2 g
Carbohydrates: 35.6 g
Fiber: 8 g
Sugar: 12.6 g
Protein: 5.5 g
Sodium: 453 mg

Eggplant Salad

Yield: 2 servings
Preparation Time: 15 minutes
Cooking Time: 3 minutes
Total Time: 18 minutes
Ingredients:
1 medium eggplant, peeled
1 small red onion, sliced
8 plum tomatoes, chopped
1 bell peppers, chopped
½ tablespoon smoked paprika
2 tablespoons lemon juice
½ cup water
1 teaspoon ground cumin
Freshly ground pepper and salt to taste
Cucumber slices for garnishing

Directions:
1. Add all the ingredients into the Instant Pot and stir.
2. Close the lid, select MANUAL, and cook at high pressure for 3 minutes.
3. When the cooking is complete, do a quick pressure release.
4. Serve over cauliflower rice or with falafels.

Nutritional Information (Per Serving)
Calories: 216
Fat: 2.2 g
Sat Fat: 0.3 g
Carbohydrates: 48.1 g
Fiber: 15.9 g
Sugar: 31.6 g
Protein: 9.7 g

Ratatouille

Yield: 4 servings
Preparation Time: 15 minutes
Cooking Time: 10 minutes
Total Time: 25 minutes
Ingredients:
1 zucchini, cubed
1 large bell pepper, chopped into squares
1 medium onion, chopped
1½ cups eggplant, cubed
3 cloves garlic, minced
Freshly ground pepper, crushed red pepper and salt to taste
2 tomatoes, chopped
2 tablespoons extra-virgin olive oil
½ teaspoon balsamic vinegar
Basil leaves to garnish
A handful fresh parsley to garnish

Directions:
1. Select SAUTÉ. Add oil and onions and sauté until translucent.

2. Add rest of the ingredients except salt, basil and parsley to the pot. Mix well. Press Cancel.

3. Close the lid, select MANUAL, and cook at high pressure for 5 minutes.

4. When the cooking is complete, do a quick pressure release.

5. Sprinkle with salt and garnish with basil and parsley, and serve.

Nutritional Information (Per Serving)
Calories: 131
Fat: 7.5 g
Sat Fat: 1 g
Carbohydrates: 16.3 g

Fiber: 6.3 g
Sugar: 8.5 g
Protein: 3 g

Garlic Green Beans

Yield: 4 servings
Preparation Time: 15 minutes
Cooking Time: 5 minutes
Total Time: 20 minutes
Ingredients:
1 pound fresh green beans
1 tablespoon olive oil
3 garlic cloves, minced
Salt and pepper to taste
1½ cups water

Directions:
1. In the pot of Instant Pot, add all ingredients and stir to combine.
2. Close the lid, select MANUAL, and cook at low pressure for 5 minutes.
3. When the cooking is complete, do a quick pressure release.
4. Serve hot.

Nutritional Information (Per Serving)
Calories: 69
Fat: 3.7 g
Sat Fat: 0.5 g
Carbohydrates: 8.8 g
Fiber: 3.9 g
Sugar: 1.6 g
Protein: 2.2 g
Sodium: 46 mg

CHAPTER SEVEN

Dessert

Poached Pears

Yield: 2 servings

Preparation Time: 10 minutes

Cooking Time: 10 minutes

Total Time: 20 minutes

Ingredients:

1½ cups red wine

6 ounces coconut sugar

1 vanilla pod

1 clove

Pinch of ground cinnamon

6 green pears

Directions:

1. At the bottom of Instant Pot, mix together all ingredients except pears.

2. Arrange pears over the wine mixture.

3. Close the lid, select MANUAL, and cook at high pressure for 10 minutes.

4. When the cooking is complete, do a quick pressure release.

5. Open the lid and transfer pears onto a serving platter. Cool for about 10 minutes.

6. Top with the wine sauce and serve.

Nutritional Information (Per Serving)
Calories: 276
Fat: 0.3 g
Sat Fat: 0 g

Carbohydrates: 61.8 g
Fiber: 6.5 g
Sugar: 49.2 g
Protein: 0.8 g
Sodium: 5 mg

Tapioca Pudding

Yield: 2 servings
Preparation Time: 10 minutes
Cooking Time: 8 minutes
Total Time: 18 minutes
Ingredients:
½ cup tapioca pearls, rinsed
¼ cup raw honey
1¾ cups unsweetened almond milk
¼ teaspoon organic vanilla extract
2 tablespoons almonds, chopped

Directions:
1. In a large heat proof bowl, add all ingredients except almonds and stir to combine well.
2. At the bottom of Instant Pot, arrange a steamer trivet and pour 1 cup of water.
3. Place the bowl on top of trivet.
4. Close the lid, select MANUAL, and cook at high pressure for 8 minutes.
5. When the cooking is complete, do a quick pressure release.
6. Let the pudding stand in the Instant Pot for about 5 minutes.
7. Stir to mix the pudding. Serve warm with the topping of almonds.

Nutritional Information (Per Serving)
Calories: 336

Fat: 6 g
Sat Fat: 0.5 g
Carbohydrates: 71.7 g
Fiber: 2 g
Sugar: 36.4 g
Protein: 4.2 g
Sodium: 160 mg

Carrot Pudding

Yield: 4 servings
Preparation Time: 15 minutes
Cooking Time: 10 minutes
Total Time: 25 minutes
Ingredients:
34 ounces unsweetened almond milk, divided
3 small carrots, peeled and chopped roughly
8 dates, pitted and chopped
½ cup unsalted cashews, toasted
½ teaspoon ground cardamom
Pinch of saffron threads, crushed
2 tablespoons pistachios, chopped

Directions:
1. In the Instant Pot, mix together 1 cup of almond milk, carrots, dates and cashews.

2. Close the lid, select MANUAL, and cook at high pressure for 7 minutes.

3. When the cooking is complete, do a quick pressure release.

4. Open the lid and keep aside to cool slightly.

5. Transfer carrot mixture to a blender and pulse until smooth.

6. Return the pureed mixture to Instant Pot and select SAUTÉ.

7. Stir in remaining almond milk, cardamom and saffron threads and cook for 2–3 minutes.

8. Press CANCEL and transfer pudding to a large serving bowl. Keep aside to cool.

9. Refrigerate to chill.

10. Garnish with pistachios and serve.

Nutritional Information (Per Serving)
Calories: 210
Fat: 12.2 g
Sat Fat: 2 g
Carbohydrates: 24.4 g
Fiber: 4.4 g
Sugar: 13.4 g
Protein: 4.7 g
Sodium: 213 mg

Pumpkin Pudding

Yield: 12 servings
Preparation Time: 10 minutes
Cooking Time: 30 minutes
Total Time: 40 minutes
Ingredients:
For pumpkin pudding:
1½ cups pureed pumpkin
2½ tablespoons pumpkin pie spice
1 cup coconut milk
2 eggs
1 cup maple syrup
1 teaspoon sea salt
4 teaspoons sustainably sourced gelatin

For coconut ginger glaze:
1½ cups coconut cream, at room temperature
⅛ teaspoon stevia
2 teaspoons ground ginger
Walnuts to top (optional)

Directions:
1. Pour coconut milk into a saucepan. Sprinkle gelatin over it.
2. Place the saucepan over medium low heat. Stir until gelatin dissolves completely. Turn off the heat.
3. Add rest of the ingredients of pudding in a bowl and whisk until well combined. Pour the milk mixture into it and mix until well combined.
4. Pour into a generously greased soufflé pan or mold. Cover with aluminum foil.
5. Place a trivet inside the Instant Pot. Pour 2 cups of water.
6. Place the pan over the trivet.

7. Close the lid, select MANUAL, and cook at high pressure for 30 minutes.

8. When the cooking is complete, use a natural pressure release.

9. Cool and chill for a few hours.

10. Mix together all the glaze ingredients (except walnuts) in a bowl.

11. Run a knife all around the edges of the pan and invert on to a plate. Spoon the glaze over the pudding. Sprinkle walnuts if using.

12. Slice and serve. It can last for 2–3 days in the refrigerator.

Nutritional Information (Per Serving)
Calories: 270
Fat: 11.8 g
Sat Fat: 10.3 g
Carbohydrates: 40.9 g
Fiber: 1.1 g
Sugar: 36 g
Protein: 2.7 g
Sodium: 188 mg

Banana Cake

Yield: 8 servings

Preparation Time: 15 minutes

Cooking Time: 30 minutes

Total Time: 45 minutes

Ingredients:

1½ cups cassava flour

½ teaspoon baking soda

1 teaspoon baking powder

Pinch of salt

¾ cup coconut sugar

⅓ cup coconut oil, softened

1 egg

1 teaspoon vanilla extract

2 ripe bananas, peeled and mashed

⅓ cup unsweetened almond milk

1½ teaspoon cream of tartar

¼ cup walnuts, chopped

Directions:

1. Grease a heat proof round pan that will fit in Instant Pot. Keep aside.

2. In a large bowl, mix together flour, baking soda, baking powder and salt.

3. In another bowl, add coconut sugar and coconut oil and beat until a creamy mixture forms.

4. Add egg, vanilla extract and banana and beat until well combined. Add milk and cream of tartar and mix well.

5. Add egg mixture into flour mixture and mix until well combined. Fold in walnuts.

6. Transfer the mixture into the prepared pan gently, pressing downwards.

7. At the bottom of Instant Pot, arrange a steamer trivet and pour 2 cups of water and 1 tablespoon of vinegar.

8. Place the pan on top of trivet.

9. Close the lid, select MANUAL, and cook at high pressure for 30 minutes.

10. When the cooking is complete, do a quick pressure release.

11. Open the lid and transfer the pan onto a wire rack to cool completely before slicing the cake.

Nutritional Information (Per Serving)
Calories: 232
Fat: 12.2 g
Sat Fat: 8.2 g
Carbohydrates: 31.2 g
Fiber: 1.3 g
Sugar: 21.8 g
Protein: 2 g
Sodium: 135 mg

Mini Chocolaty Cakes

Yield: 3 servings
Preparation Time: 15 minutes
Cooking Time: 30 minutes
Total Time: 45 minutes
Ingredients:
1 green plantain, peeled
½ ripe banana, peeled
¼ cup avocado, peeled, pitted and chopped
2 tablespoons raw honey
2 tablespoons coconut oil, melted
2 tablespoons cacao powder
½ teaspoon apple cider vinegar
¾ teaspoon baking soda
⅛ teaspoon cream of tartar

Directions:
1. In a food processor, add all ingredients and pulse until smooth
2. Place the mixture into 3 lightly grease ramekins evenly.
3. At the bottom of Instant Pot, arrange a steamer trivet and pour 1 cup of water.
4. Place the ramekins on top of the trivet.
5. Close the lid, select MANUAL, and cook at high pressure for 18 minutes.
6. When the cooking is complete, do a natural pressure release for 10 minutes. Quick release the remaining pressure.
7. Serve warm.

Nutritional Information (Per Serving)
Calories: 367
Fat: 13.3 g
Sat Fat: 4.2 g
Carbohydrates: 56.8 g

Fiber: 5.6 g
Sugar: 34.4 g
Protein: 2.2 g
Sodium: 470 mg

Chocolate Cake

Yield: 6 servings
Preparation Time: 15 minutes
Cooking Time: 7 minutes
Total Time: 22 minutes
Ingredients:
2/3 cup 70% chocolate, chopped
½ cup applesauce
2 eggs
1 teaspoon organic vanilla extract
¼ cup arrowroot starch
3 tablespoons unsweetened cocoa powder plus more for dusting
Pinch of salt

Directions:
1. At the bottom of Instant Pot, arrange a steamer trivet and pour 2 cups of water.
2. Place the chocolate into a ramekin.
3. Place the ramekin on top of the trivet.
4. Select SAUTÉ and cook for 2–3 minutes, until the chocolate melts.
5. Press CANCEL and remove the ramekin.
6. In a bowl, add applesauce, eggs, and vanilla extract and beat until well combined.
7. Add arrowroot, cocoa powder and salt and gently, stir to combine well.

8. Stir in melted chocolate.

9. Generously grease a 6-inch cake pan and then, dust with extra cocoa powder.

10. Place the cake mixture into the prepared cake pan evenly.

11. Place the cake pan on top of the trivet.

12. Close the lid, select MANUAL, and cook at high pressure for 4 minutes.

13. When the cooking is complete, use a natural pressure release.

14. Open the lid and transfer the cake pan to a wire rack to cool for about 10 minutes.

15. Carefully invert the cake onto rack to cool completely before serving.

Nutritional Information (Per Serving)
Calories: 156
Fat: 7.4 g
Sat Fat: 4.6 g
Carbohydrates: 19.7 g
Fiber: 1.9 g
Sugar: 11.9 g
Protein: 3.8 g
Sodium: 63 mg

Fudge

Yield: 10 servings
Preparation Time: 10 minutes
Cooking Time: 20 minutes
Total Time: 30 minutes
Ingredients:
1¼ cups nondairy dark chocolate chips
2 tablespoons coconut sugar
A pinch of sea salt
½ teaspoon vanilla extract
¼ cup canned coconut milk
1 tablespoon coconut oil

Directions:
1. Add 2 cups water into the Instant Pot and set a trivet inside.
2. In a bowl, add all the ingredients and mix well.
3. Transfer the mixture into a greased ovenproof dish. Cover with foil.
4. Place the dish on the trivet.
5. Close the lid and cook for 20 minutes at high pressure.
6. When the cooking is complete, use a natural pressure release.
7. Once it has cooled, remove the dish.
8. Refrigerate until the fudge is set.

Nutritional Information (Per Serving)
Calories: 179
Fat: 10.8 g
Sat Fat: 8.5 g
Carbohydrates: 23.8 g
Fiber: 0.1 g
Sugar: 19.7 g
Protein: 2.2 g
Sodium: 24 mg

Instant Pot Paleo Mug Cake

Yield: 3 servings
Preparation Time: 5 minutes
Cooking Time: 10 minutes
Total Time: 15 minutes
Ingredients:
2/3 cup almond flour
2 tablespoons maple syrup
¼ teaspoon salt
2 eggs
1 teaspoon vanilla extract

Directions:
1. Add all the ingredients into a bowl and whisk until well combined.
2. Spoon into 2–4 masons' jars. Fill up to 2/3.
3. Pour 1 cup water in the Instant Pot. Place a trivet in it. Cover the jars with foil.
4. Place the mason's jar on the trivet.
5. Close the lid, select MANUAL, and cook at high pressure for 10 minutes.
6. When the cooking is complete, do a quick pressure release.
7. Cool and serve either warm or cold.

Nutritional Information (Per Serving)
Calories: 118
Fat: 5.9 g
Sat Fat: 1.1 g
Carbohydrates: 10.7 g
Fiber: 0.7 g
Sugar: 8.3 g
Protein: 5 g
Sodium: 238 mg

Coconut Banana Foster

Yield: 8 servings
Preparation Time: 10 minutes
Cooking Time: 2 hours 15 minutes
Total Time: 2 hours 25 minutes
Ingredients:
8 medium firm bananas, cut into 2 inch pieces
⅛ teaspoon cloves powder
¼ teaspoon nutmeg powder
1 teaspoon cinnamon powder
6 tablespoons honey
2 tablespoons coconut oil, melted
2 tablespoons lemon juice
Coconut cream for serving (optional)

Directions:
1. Mix together all the ingredients except bananas in the Instant Pot and stir.

2. Place the bananas in the pot. Stir until the bananas are well coated with the mixture.

3. Select SLOW COOK, and cook for 1½ to 2 hours depending on how you like the consistency of the bananas to be.

4. To serve, transfer on to individual serving plates. Pour some coconut cream on top of the bananas and serve.

Nutritional Information (Per Serving)
Calories: 184
Fat: 3.9 g
Sat Fat: 3.1 g
Carbohydrates: 40.3 g
Fiber: 3.3 g
Sugar: 27.5 g
Protein: 1.4 g
Sodium: 3 mg

Conclusion

Adopting the Paleo diet takes some adjustment to your eating habits. I hope you enjoy the yummy Paleo Instant Pot recipes in this book!

Finally, I want to thank you for reading my book. If you enjoyed the book, please take the time to share your thoughts and post a review on the book retailer's website. It would be greatly appreciated!

Best wishes,

Lindsey Page